REVOLUTIONARY
and IMPERIAL
FRANCE 1750-1815

Although the fall of the Bastille has been much reinterpreted by historians, it remains the great symbolic act of the French Revolution. From the Musée Carnavelet, Paris. Used by permission of J. E. Bulloz, Paris.

REVOLUTIONARY and IMPERIAL FRANCE 1750-1815

Ernest John Knapton

Maps by Robert Sugar

CHARLES SCRIBNER'S SONS · NEW YORK

239735

Printed in the United States of America
Library of Congress Catalog Card Number 76-181037
SBN   684-12718-0 (trade cloth)
SBN   684-12717-2 (trade paper, SUL)

To my Wife

PREFACE

This work comprises chapters 14 to 20 of the author's FRANCE—AN INTERPRETIVE HISTORY, published in 1971. The importance of the period extending from 1750 to 1815 hardly needs stressing; it is hoped that the brief treatment here offered will be useful as a coherent and up-to-date account of these critical years. A new introduction, conclusion, and index have been provided and some slight additions made to chapter 6.

ERNEST JOHN KNAPTON

Chatham, Massachusetts
July, 1971

CONTENTS

x

ILLUSTRATIONS

MAPS

REVOLUTIONARY
and IMPERIAL
FRANCE 1750-1815

INTRODUCTION

The age of the French Revolution and Napoleon possesses a certain historical unity, and as the huge collections in the great libraries of the world and the steady expansion of diverse forms of research abundantly testify, it has never failed to attract attention. Although the division of history into neatly defined periods may to some degree be arbitrary and subjective, it is indisputable that in human affairs there are times of rapid, revolutionary change alternating with longer periods of stability. The *ancien régime*, a term that could be applied to much more than eighteenth-century France, was one such period of supposed stability. The ensuing age of revolution brought about basic changes whose effects have been manifest down to our own day—again, it must be stressed, in areas far wider than France itself.

The present survey outlines the essentials of this dramatic period, which can still claim much relevance for us who live in an even greater age of upheaval. We, too, hear the clamor of revolution in the troubled world which has emerged from the generally stable background of the nineteenth century. In that now vanished era many confidently believed that freedom, in Tennyson's phrase, would slowly broaden down from precedent to precedent. Human progress, as many also had held in the eighteenth century, would be orderly, civilized, and presumably unlimited.

The creation of an explosive situation in France has been variously explained: a near breakdown of the administrative and especially the financial machinery of the state; the continued assertion of privilege both by the monarchy and by a substantial section of the nobility and church; the "natural rights" crusade of the philosophes; the resentments of the economically thriving but socially and politically frustrated bourgeoisie; a deep peasant unrest; a rise in prices and recurrent near-famine conditions affecting both the countryside and the towns; the example of England and America; and even the alleged conspiracy of a few recklessly wicked men or groups within France. The crisis may well be regarded as resulting in greater or less degree from a combination of all these forces. By following the various threads it should be possible to find some acceptable meaning and intelligibility in the tangled skein of events marking the turbulent years of revolutionary change.

Even today historians are not in full agreement as to the permanent and constructive achievements of this age. The leaders of 1789 would for the most part have considered themselves reformers rather than revolutionaries. Only with the passage of time and with the emergence of armed resistance at home and abroad did the Revolution enter its more violent stage. Some of the changes then made were transient, others were to be permanent. As the fires of revolution gradually subsided, most of the basic work of the years 1789–1791 remained, to be given a more extensive and more disciplined form under the strong hand of Napoleon.

The impact of the Revolution abroad was only less significant than its impact upon France. First the newly emerged leaders of the Revolution, with their goal of the "natural frontiers" and their slogan, "War to the thrones, peace to the cottages," and then the dominating figure of Napoleon made the dramatic transformation occurring in France a powerful solvent of outworn institutions abroad. To see Napoleon simply as a military conqueror is to ignore his tremendous organizing abilities and to minimize the extent to which he was the product and heir of the French Revolution. His decision, for example, to terminate the thousand-year history of the Holy Roman Empire is but one of the many examples of his consuming desire to regard himself as the man of destiny acting out his role upon a world stage.

Though the continental countries were forced to accept a large degree of revolutionary change, they later and in increasing measure organized an opposition. Massive military force became the determinant. In 1814 and 1815—and not only in France—an age of restoration was the successor to an age of revolution. Yet, whatever significance one attaches to the fall of Napoleon, the crumbling of his vast Empire, and the return of France to its historic monarchy and its ancient limits, one fact remains indisputable: the world of the Restoration could not be simply a return to 1789.

I

THE EMERGING CRISIS
1750–1774

France at Mid-Century

Increased difficulties confronted France as it passed the mid-century mark. During the preceding War of the Austrian Succession it had, in traditional fashion, fought the Hapsburgs. Eight years after the war ended, a dramatic diplomatic revolution was to reverse the historic system and ally France with Austria against the massive power of Prussia, while at the same time it fought a colonial war of worldwide dimensions with Britain. The outcome of this Seven Years' War gravely weakened the French monarchy.

Within France administrative problems continued. While Louis XIV had been able to impose his will upon the cumbersome machinery of the autocratic monarchy, Louis XV proved increasingly incapable of directing affairs with a strong royal hand. His ministers, largely competent and even dedicated men, were unable either to make the existing machinery work or to provide an effective substitute for it. One ominous aspect was the continued unwillingness of the Parlement of Paris and the provincial parlements to surrender their privileges as a class and to accept the kind of reforms that would truly have reduced the financial and social problems of France to manageable proportions. While not reaching the point of absolute deadlock or of revolutionary crisis, domestic difficulties clearly were growing to such an extent as to leave a staggering burden for Louis XV's successor.

At the same time a remarkable spirit of criticism began to take shape among a brilliant group of writers, the *philosophes*. These men within a short span of a few decades produced a body of writings rarely if ever equaled for so much challenging thought concentrated in so brief a time. The Enlightenment was, to be sure, a European rather than a uniquely French phenomenon and had its roots in an earlier age. Yet France in this respect now occupied the center of the stage. Few historians would be disposed to see in such intellectual developments the cause of the French Revolution, for so large a transformation of political and social life must take into account far more complex forces. Even so, ideas were being accepted in important circles, including even to some extent members of the privileged classes, that were incompatible with the assumptions and practices of the Bourbon monarchy. In this sense the mid-century decades were of critical importance.

Foreign Affairs: The Weakening of France

The mutual restoration of conquests (save for Frederick II's acquisition of Silesia) which had been the general basis of the Peace of Aix-la-Chapelle in 1748 meant that France had emerged from seven years of intermittent war with nothing to show for its exertions, save possibly the heavy territorial blow dealt by Prussia to its traditional enemy Austria. Now that Frederick II clearly had made Prussia a power to be reckoned with, the old pattern of alliances could be expected to undergo important changes. This was the significant aspect of the years of peace which preceded the outbreak of another war destined to do grave damage to France.

Certain rivalries continued unchanged. Prussia's capture of Silesia and its seeming determination to dominate German affairs left Austria wholly unreconciled. Here remained one basic antagonism. The colonial duel between England and France created a second, although the command of Louis XV to his envoys that they carry out the peace negotiations at Aix-la-Chapelle "royally and not in merchant fashion" suggested a serious underestimation of the economic importance of these overseas questions. Even while at peace in Europe, England and France pursued their rivalries

◀ BUST OF VOLTAIRE, BY HOUDON *The bust, now in the Petit Palais and made by France's greatest portrait sculptor, perfectly recaptures the character of its subject.*

in the New World. French Canada continued to push its forts and trading posts beyond the Great Lakes. (See map, p. 10) An expedition sent in 1749 claimed the Ohio Valley in the name of Louis XV, establishing Fort Duquesne in 1753 at what is now Pittsburgh. In the same year prominent British and Virginia merchants organized the Ohio Company to develop half a million acres of land near the upper Ohio River. A young Virginia officer, George Washington, went over the Alleghenies in 1753 hoping to establish a title to the Ohio Valley, but he was obliged in 1754 to surrender his small force to the French, returning to Virginia under a year's parole. General Braddock's expedition of 1755 met disaster trying to fight a frontier war according to European military techniques. In the same year the British removed the remaining French in Nova Scotia (the Acadians) to scattered homes in the American colonies and Louisiana. The total expulsions, known as the *Grand Dérangement*, are estimated to have numbered ten thousand. On the high seas some three hundred French merchant ships were seized by the Royal Navy.

At the same time a struggle of equal significance was developing in India. (See map, P. 10) Here a young servant of the British East India Company, Robert Clive, demonstrated extraordinary genius as a leader and general. His French opponent was Joseph Dupleix, who became governor general in 1751 with a policy of winning the favor of local rulers and building up a native sepoy army in southern India. He might well have succeeded in bringing this part of the subcontinent under French control, for by 1753 Dupleix held a territory twice as large as France. It had become apparent, however, that his government wished a policy of peace at almost any price and in the following year he was recalled. Clive won a series of spectacular victories at Arcot, Calcutta, and Plassey, so that by the time England and France became embroiled again in European war the future of France's remaining Indian possessions was gravely threatened.

The Diplomatic Revolution of 1756 in Europe dissolved the antagonism between France and the House of Hapsburg that had been basic for over two hundred years. This has, indeed, been described as the greatest of all diplomatic revolutions. It must be examined in order to see how it was brought about, and even more for what it accomplished. The point of critical uncertainty for France, although engaged in a colonial war involving both India and North America, still lay in Europe. Granted France's basic rivalry with Great Britain, was it essential that the historic opposition to Austria should remain unaltered? This was the problem which also presented itself to Count Kaunitz, the brilliant statesman who became chancellor and foreign minister to Maria Theresa in 1753. To him the great dangers presented by the powerful state of Prussia meant that Austria must adopt a new policy of alliance.

As early as 1749 Kaunitz had sought to persuade Maria Theresa that France should be won away from Prussia, though tentative efforts in this direction made by him as envoy at Versailles were at first rebuffed. Britain, meanwhile, had been unable to obtain a promise of help from Austria for the defense of Hanover. In 1755 Kaunitz opened a vigorous campaign, his technique being to have the Austrian ambassador at Versailles work through the Marquise de Pompadour and her close friend the abbé Bernis. Though these were the intermediaries, there is no doubt that Louis XV made the major decisions. He had no confidence at all in his supposed ally Frederick II who had twice withdrawn from the Silesian War and whom he regarded as an upstart and infidel.

Kaunitz's plans became a reality as the result of moves coming from Great Britain. This country was nervous, as always, about a possible French encroachment in the Low Countries and also, since a Hanoverian ruler was now upon the English throne, about the integrity of the electorate of Hanover. The outcome was the Convention of Westminster in January 1756, a mutual agreement of Britain and Prussia to oppose the entrance into Germany of any foreign troops. This agreement also had the consequence of causing a breach in the understanding between Britain and Russia. Regarding Prussia's action as "a base desertion," Louis XV now ordered his ministers to accept the overtures from Austria. The Treaty of Versailles, signed in May 1756, pledged both signatories to mutual defense if attacked in Europe. Thus, despite the long tradition of Hapsburg-Bourbon rivalry, France and Austria were now allied and soon were standing also with Russia against the Protestant powers of Great Britain and Prussia.

The Seven Years' War became a reality when in August Frederick II suddenly invaded his neighbor Saxony. Austria and France soon signed a Second Treaty of Versailles (May 1757), much more sweeping and specific in its terms than the first treaty. France agreed to put an army of 100,000 men in the field against Prussia and provide subsidies of twelve million livres. As soon as Austria should regain Silesia this power agreed to turn over the greater part of the Austrian Netherlands to Don Philip, the second son of Elizabeth Farnese, Austria regaining Parma and Piacenza. A few border towns would go to France. Most striking was the commitment by France to join with Austria in dismembering the Prussian state put together so arduously by Frederick II and his predecessors. The sweeping phrase in the French text was "*la destruction totale de la Prusse.*" The large significance of what happened is clear. Frederick's actions led

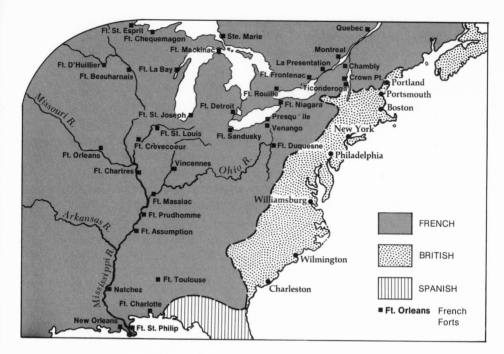

BRITISH AND FRENCH IN NORTH AMERICA, 1755

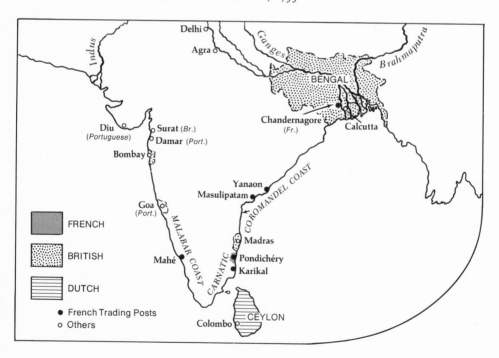

FRENCH AND BRITISH POWER IN INDIA, 1763

him to walk into a trap set for him by Kaunitz. The French situation has been well put by one of the most acute students of this period:

> The supreme irony of Kaunitz's policy lay in the success
> with which he had jockeyed France into trying to restore
> Austria literally to that position in Germany from which all
> French statesmen since Richelieu had been attempting to
> expel her. Incapable of continuing Louis XIV's policy of
> continental hegemony, France had lapsed into the position of
> a vassal state of Austria.[1]

The war in Europe can be briefly described. Frederick II, getting little aid from Britain and ringed by the hostile coalition of Austria, France, Russia, and Sweden, won nevertheless his brilliant victories at Rossbach, Leuthen, and Zorndorf. He could not prevent a Russian army from entering and ravaging the suburbs of Berlin, nearly two hundred years before the holocaust of Hitler's last days, and in 1759 he met near disaster at Kunersdorf. The French began the war with the capture of Minorca from the English. Yet though they forced the duke of Cumberland to capitulate and to abandon Hanover, they soon frittered away their successes. Factional rivalries at home made impossible any clear direction of the war, and the French, having been defeated once at Rossbach, were routed again at Minden. On the sea the action was more vigorous and for a time England was faced with the prospect of an actual French invasion. In response the British blockaded French ports all the way from Dunkirk to Toulon, and in 1759 Admiral Hawke smashed a French fleet at Quiberon Bay, thus ending the invasion danger.

The true rivalry of France and England revealed itself in the war overseas. When William Pitt entered the Newcastle cabinet in 1757, he became largely responsible for prosecuting the war. In North America Louisbourg which had been returned to the French in 1748 was recaptured in 1758, soon to be followed by Ticonderoga, Fort Frontenac, Fort Niagara, Fort Duquesne, and other important points. In 1759 General Wolfe led his Highlanders up from the St. Lawrence River to the Plains of Abraham and won Quebec. This was in truth the year of disasters for France. In the next year the capture of Montreal meant the end of French Canada. In the West Indies the British seized Martinique, Guadeloupe, Grenada, St. Vincent, and St. Lucia, as well as Senegal and Gorée on the African coast. In India the struggle that had begun during the War of the Austrian

[1] Walter Dorn, *Competition for Empire, 1740–1763* (1940), p. 313.

Succession reached the point of disaster for France when in 1761 the British captured Pondichéry.

A series of incompetent ministers in France failed to give the leadership so sorely needed. One controller general of finances by the name of Silhouette is remembered less for his financial efforts than for having his name identified with the outlines of portraits, filled in with black, that became so popular around the mid-century. The abbé Bernis withdrew from public affairs, being rewarded with a cardinal's hat. Finally, another protégé of Madame de Pompadour, the duke of Choiseul, was made secretary of state for foreign affairs. Though Choiseul could not win the war, by the celebrated *pacte de famille* of 1761 he succeeded in linking together the Bourbon rulers of France, Spain, Naples, and Parma and brought Spain into the war on the French side. The death of Empress Elizabeth of Russia in 1762 removed one of Frederick II's bitterest and most dangerous opponents and made the prospect of peace more likely. Thus negotiations could be undertaken to end a war which no one wished to see continue longer.

The Peace of Paris in 1763 confirmed England's colonial victory over France. The latter's most sweeping losses were in the New World, where it gave up all its Canadian possessions, keeping only the two tiny fishing islands of St. Pierre and Miquelon, which to this day remain French. This was the end of an era. As the price for joining the war in 1761, Spain obtained the Louisiana territory west of the Mississippi, giving the Floridas to Britain. All French territory east of the Mississippi was ceded to Britain. In the West Indies France recovered Martinique and Guadeloupe, obtaining also St. Lucia, while Great Britain won St. Vincent, Dominica, and Tobago. On the African coast France got back the island of Gorée. In India the French held only six trading posts, on the condition that they dismantle their defenses. Since the French East India Company was abolished in 1769 and its business taken over by the crown, France's few Indian possessions were henceforth administered simply as colonies.

The almost simultaneous Peace of Hubertsburg between Austria and Prussia left the latter in full possession of Silesia. During the war Prussia had suffered terrible losses—an estimated 500,000 out of a total population of 4,500,000. Despite near disaster it was still territorially well established and had so strong an army that France could no longer pretend to be the arbiter of Europe. It is clear that the results of the Seven Years' War gravely shook the French monarchy and helped in some degree to prepare for its downfall. Though France retained the link with Austria, and indeed strengthened it by the marriage of the future Louis XVI to Marie Antoinette, it is significant that when war came again in 1792 France's opponents were to be both Prussia and Austria, and that the first great achievement of France's republican armies was to be the capture of the Austrian Netherlands. Ultimately the French Republic was to prove itself capable of what the monarchy never had been able to achieve.

Domestic Problems in the Last Decade of Louis XV

The last decade of Louis XV's reign illustrates perfectly both the continuing problems which beset his reign and the inadequacy of the efforts to meet them. Choiseul had brought his country out of the Seven Years' War; in 1766 the death of Stanislas Leszczinski made the duchy of Lorraine a part of France, its most notable gain since the Peace of Utrecht. In 1768 Corsica, in revolt from Genoa, was bought for two million livres, one year before the birth there of an infant then known in the Corsican dialect as Napoleone Buonaparte.

Choiseul's plans for reform, though admired by the philosophes, did not succeed. The *vingtième*, supposedly a tax of one-twentieth imposed in 1749 on all land and personal property, had been repudiated by the clergy, and despite renewals in 1756 and 1760 it was successfully evaded by the other privileged classes. Year by year the government was responsible for increased deficits, borrowing at higher rates, and failure to meet interest payments on its bonds. Choiseul also tried to revitalize trade with France's remaining colonies, and he was successful in building the navy to double its size. He sought to reform the army, especially in establishing a separate artillery corps which reached a high level of technical efficiency. He was not strong enough, however, to cope with the steady resistance of the parlements to his fiscal demands.

Though Choiseul was not the initiator of it, a significant move was made in another field. The Jesuit order had lost its favored position with the monarchy, and because of its disciplined obedience to Rome it had incurred the hostility of the Parlement of Paris. In 1762 a decree of the Parlement ordered the abolition of the Society of Jesus in France and the confiscation of its possessions on the ground that its doctrines were "perverse, destructive of all principles of religion, and even of honesty, injurious to Christian morality, pernicious to civil society, seditious, hostile to the rights of the nation and the power of the king." This was confirmed two years later by a royal edict. Such action was the parallel to similar moves in other countries and anticipated the formal suppression of the entire Order by the papacy in 1773.

The political storms eventually proved too much for Choiseul who in the eyes of Louis XV seemed too subservient to the parlements. The opposition of the Parlement of Paris and the corresponding provincial bodies arose from their essentially selfish nature. They were the spokesmen of a privileged administrative class, the nobility of the robe, ready to associate themselves with the equally selfish interests of the greater nobility. Resistance to fiscal demands arising from the wars became particularly vocal in the parlement of Brittany and led to a long conflict there. Though Louis XV had given a stinging rebuke to the Parlement of Paris in 1766 with the words, "It is in my person alone that the sovereign power resides . . . and the rights and interests of the nation . . . are necessarily joined with mine and rest only in my hands," he was unable to quell the storm. Choiseul was beset by many dangers. The Marquise de Pompadour had died in 1764, and her eventual successor, the empty-headed, vulgar beauty, Madame du Barry, whom Choiseul held in contempt worked against him. This was especially true when in 1770 Choiseul's diplomatic policy brought Marie Antoinette to France as the bride of the dauphin. This Hapsburg princess found it hard to make obeisance to the king's new *maîtresse en titre*, for Madame du Barry was a shop girl having risen almost literally from the streets. Choiseul's dismissal at the end of the year came at a time of renewed crisis with the parlements.

The new triumvirate of Maupeou as chancellor, Terray as controller general, and d'Aiguillon as foreign secretary precipitated the last crisis of the reign and pointed ominously to the future. An open rejection by the Parlement of Paris of the king's demands led to the exile from Paris of 130 magistrates in 1771, followed by similar action against the provincial parlements. In their place new courts were set up, and the vast jurisdiction of the Parlement of Paris was divided among six new bodies, all appointed by the crown. The sale of legal offices was to be abolished and justice was to be made free to all. Amid the confused protests against the "Maupeou parlements" Louis XV fell ill of smallpox in 1774 and died unmourned, leaving the monarchy discredited and all the great problems of reform unsolved.

Mobilization of Criticism: The Philosophes

The last half of the reign of Louis XV was *par excellence* the period of the Enlightenment, when the philosophes produced a body of critical literature notable both for the distinction of its style and for the power of its ideas. The precise impact of this literature upon public events must remain a question for debate; its originality and richness are beyond question.

The Enlightenment had historic roots reaching back to the seventeenth century, and it was the common property of men of ideas throughout a much wider area than merely France. D'Alembert's sketch of its development in the "Preliminary Discourse" which he wrote for Diderot's *Encyclopedia* began significantly with the great English chancellor of Elizabethan and Jacobean times, Francis Bacon. And it was to be a German, Immanuel Kant, who in 1784 answered the question, "What is Enlightenment?" by the famous declaration that it is the emergence of man from his self-imposed tutelage.

One can properly single out an early period of the French Enlightenment associated with two great names, famous before the mid-century had been reached and notable both in France and abroad for their profound and continuing influence.[2] Montesquieu, a baron and a member of the administrative nobility, crowned his earlier writings with the famous *Spirit of the Laws*, published in 1748 seven years before his death. Voltaire covered a much wider span. His youthful play, *Oedipus*, was published in 1718 at the beginning of a literary career that was to continue ever more spectacularly for sixty years. His *Philosophical Letters on the English* had appeared at Paris in 1733. Unlike Montesquieu, Voltaire lived on through the central period of the Enlightenment, a time crowded with new names, and his final apotheosis came in 1778 when on his return to Paris after twenty-eight years of living on the Swiss frontier he was crowned with laurels at the Comédie Française, within weeks of his death. A third generation of the Enlightenment, reaching to the eve of the French Revolution, was marked by the names of Holbach, Turgot, and Condorcet.

A striking feature of the 1750s and the 1760s was the close association of men who knew each other well, men such as Diderot, Condillac, Helvétius, D'Alembert, and La Mettrie. Despite their many disagreements, these philosophes could truly be called a band of brothers. Their activities were notably helped by a newly popular social feature of the age, the salon. The seventeenth-century salon of Madame de Rambouillet had been almost unique; now great hostesses such as Madame du Deffand, Madame Geoffrin, Julie de l'Espinasse, Madame d'Epinay, and Madame Necker not only welcomed the writers of talent but themselves contributed to the flow of wit and ideas. Coffeehouses and theaters were similar centers of ferment. The publication of books and newspapers was little impeded by a censorship that was at the same time inefficient and benign. If need be, books printed in Holland or England could easily be smuggled into France and sold under a false imprint. The jurist Malesherbes who was in charge of

[2] See R. Shackleton, *Montesquieu* (1961), and Peter Gay, *Voltaire's Politics* (1958).

the censorship showed himself so tolerant of the philosophes that he could almost be considered to be one of them. In such an atmosphere the mutual stimulation arising from new ideas was inevitable.

The Enlightenment can be defined in one basic sense as an attempt to free the human mind from long centuries of enslavement to authority of all kinds. This explains its scorn for the Middle Ages, for feudal institutions, for scholasticism, for what was considered to be religious obscurantism, and even for Gothic architecture and the poetry of Dante. It would be wrong to charge the philosophes with having a contempt for all history; rather, in their view of the past they envisaged the medieval world as a long period of darkness on the other side of which they admired the rationalism and science of Greece and Rome. The famous example of Madame Roland who boasted of having in her youth carried a copy of Plutarch to church instead of a prayer book neatly illustrates the point. In sum, what the philosophes sought was to be free from the dead hand of the past—in Diderot's phrase, "to change the general manner of thinking" (*changer la façon commune de penser*). "Everything," he wrote in another connection, "must be examined, everything must be shaken up, without exception and without circumspection."

The positive side of the Enlightenment was based on the rejection of the idea of all-embracing philosophic systems and a firm acceptance of the models and patterns of contemporary science. Here the debt to England was enormous. The names of "le grand Locke" and "le grand Newton" had been familiar since the time of Voltaire's *Philosophical Letters*. The Enlightenment approach to knowledge was that of the empiricism of John Locke, who held that all knowledge must be derived primarily from sense experience. "We must never make hypotheses," Voltaire wrote in his *Treatise on Metaphysics;*

> we must never say: Let us begin by inventing principles according to which we attempt to explain everything. We should say rather: Let us make an exact analysis of things. . . . When we cannot utilize the compass of mathematics or the torch of experience and physics, it is certain that we cannot take a single step forward.

The method of the philosophes could never be divorced from its practical application. Here again Diderot clearly made the point:

> The magistrate deals out justice; the philosopher teaches the magistrate what is just and unjust. The soldier defends

his country; the philosopher teaches the soldier what a
fatherland is. The priest recommends to his people the love
and respect of the gods; the philosopher teaches the priest
what the gods are. The sovereign commands all; the
philosopher teaches the sovereign the origins and limits
of his authority. Every man has duties to his family and his
society; the philosopher teaches everyone what these
duties are. Man is exposed to misfortune and pain; the
philosopher teaches man how to suffer.

The philosophes were never more united than in their attacks upon
organized religion and upon conventional Christian teaching. So much is
this true that one of the most distinguished of contemporary scholars of
the Enlightenment has used the phrase, "The Rise of Modern Paganism,"
as the subtitle for the first volume of his brilliant study.[3] This may be to
say too much. Yet, whether one identifies the various writers as deists,
materialists, or atheists, the crusading spirit was always there. Voltaire's
outrage at the solid backing given by the civil authorities to an intolerant
Church was most eloquently shown in his denunciation of the Calas affair,
a case where Jean Calas, a respectable Protestant of Toulouse, had been
tortured and executed, supposedly and almost certainly unjustifiably for
the murder of a son who had accepted the Catholic faith. Professor Gay
has made it clear that Voltaire's attacks were not simply directed against
the intolerance of the Church, but were part of "a distaste for Christianity
amounting almost to an obsession." Voltaire died in 1778 refusing the
ministrations of a priest.

The currents of materialism ran very strongly. La Mettrie's *Man a
Machine* (1747) had used the evidence of physiology to argue that man
was a pure mechanism. He could be regarded equally well as a plant, an
animal, or a machine—a being in whom all mental processes were the outcome of nothing more than physical forces. "Let us conclude boldly," he
wrote, "that man is a machine, and that in the whole universe there is but
a single substance with various modifications." Condillac's *Treatise on
Sensations* (1754) held that if we could take a statue and endow it with the
sense of sight, we would have a statue that could see; endow it with hear-
ing, and we would have a statue that could see and hear; endow it with all
five senses, and we would have a man. Helvétius expounded such complete materialism in his *On the Mind* (1759) that even Voltaire was
shocked. Baron Holbach's *System of Nature* (1770) argued that the idea

[3] Peter Gay, *The Enlightenment: An Interpretation. I, The Rise of Modern Paganism* (1967).

of God arises only "in ignorance, fear, and calamity." To discover the principles of morality, Holbach wrote later, "men have no need of theology, or revelation, or of gods; they need only common sense."

Much of the political ideology of the philosophes was based on the admiration for British institutions which had been put forward in the writings of Montesquieu and Voltaire. The concept of a natural law and a rational order made welcome Locke's notion that all men, even in the state of nature, were endowed with certain natural rights which it is the purpose of governments to guarantee. It remained for Rousseau's unique genius to formulate the basic concepts of democracy; some of the philosophes would probably have settled for a truly enlightened despotism as the best means of achieving the goals they desired. Yet Montesquieu's *Spirit of the Laws* had propounded his famous threefold classification of states into despotisms, of which the principle is fear; monarchies, of which the principle is honor; and republics, of which the ordering principle is virtue. And Voltaire's *Candide* (1759), the most devastating of all morality tales, said of France: "Imagine all the contradictions, all the possible incompatibilities, you will find them in the government, in the law courts, in the churches, and in the theaters of this oddity among the nations."

Another acute interest of the philosophes was human welfare and social betterment, closely associated with their acceptance of the doctrine of progress and their belief in the perfectibility of man. If happiness is to be attained here on earth, then there is a common responsibility to see that this happiness is shared. Fontenelle's brief *Digression on the Ancients and the Moderns* of 1688 had insisted on the steady progress visible in modern times, as did the abbé Saint-Pierre's *Observations on the Continual Progress of Universal Reason* of 1737 and Turgot's *Discourses on Universal History* of 1750. Such works, indicating what might be, and indeed what in time would be, served more as an indirect criticism of the inefficient monarchy than as any actual blueprint of reform.

Among the original thinkers of this period the Physiocrats hold an important place. They chose to refer to themselves as "the Economists," and one of their number Pierre Dupont de Nemours later devised for them the term *Physiocrat*, meaning a ruler of nature. These writers were important for the questions they asked. What is the source of a nation's wealth, and how are wealth and welfare to be stimulated? Certainly not by the manipulation of a balance of trade or by simply hoarding gold. In the end, the well-being of a state will be measured by the excess of the annual product over its cost. The unjust and inefficient system of taxation in France and the cumbersome network of internal tolls and tariffs were doing great harm. Agriculture above all must be given the greatest freedom and encouragement, for from the soil ultimately the nation's wealth will come.

The peerless leader of the Physiocratic group was a court physician, François Quesnay, whom Louis XV was pleased to call "my philosopher" and who was known to his followers as "the Confucius of the West." His *Tableau économique* (1758) held that the laws of economics were as demonstrable as those of algebra or geometry. The wise legislator (a favorite phrase) will see to it that the farmer is free to increase his wealth and thereby contribute to the general well-being of society. Trade and manufacture are "useful," but "sterile," for they do not add fundamentally to the world's wealth. "It is agriculture," Quesnay wrote, "which furnishes the material of industry and commerce, and pays for both." By complicated tables he tried to show that the surplus created by agriculture—the "net product"—flowed through the economy in such a way as to enrich it in every aspect.[4] To meet the needs of the state a single direct tax should be imposed upon land. In this way the chaos of taxes, tolls, feudal dues, and excises would be swept away under the general principle of *laissez faire, laissez passer*—"leave things alone."

Another distinguished Physiocrat, Turgot, served ably for a time as intendant of the province of Limoges and subsequently for two years as controller general of finances. In 1766 Turgot wrote for the benefit of two Chinese students his *Reflections on the Formation and Distribution of Wealth* containing the standard Physiocratic argument that land is the only true source of wealth and that only its net product should be taxed. It followed that industry and commerce should be left alone. The anticipation of the ideas of Adam Smith is clear.

The versatile genius of Voltaire made him, more than any of his colleagues, an innovator in the field of historical writing. In 1751 he published his *Age of Louis XIV* in which he analyzed the Great Age from the varied viewpoints of institutions, politics, wars, art, music, letters, and society. Voltaire praised not so much the power of Louis XIV as the rich achievements of the era: "I shall try to paint for posterity not the actions of one man," he wrote, "but the spirit of the men of the most enlightened age of all time." Shortly afterwards in his *Essay on the Manners and Spirit of the Nations* (1754) Voltaire undertook to sketch the general evolution of culture from Charlemagne to Louis XIII. In fourteen introductory chapters he first attempted a grand survey of history from primitive times

---

[4] One of Quesnay's most ardent contemporary admirers ranked the *Tableau économique* with the invention of writing and the invention of money as the three greatest discoveries since the world began. A modern scholar, Sir Alexander Gray, calls it "a vast mystification."

which encompassed the civilizations of China, Persia, Arabia, and the classical world. The search for something larger than a political narrative and the attempt to explain the origins of religion and other institutions give permanent brilliance to a work which, if judged by conventional historical standards, would prove gravely defective.

History can easily become propaganda, never more so than in the eighteenth century. The Abbé Raynal's ponderously entitled *Philosophical and Political History of the Establishments and the Commerce of Europeans in the Two Indies* (1770) had more fine phrases about natural rights and liberty than it had history, although it did, to be sure, employ a substantial body of statistical material to make its points. Its popularity led to numerous subsequent editions; it also caused the work to be banned in France and burned by the public executioner.

Diderot's great *Encyclopedia* best exemplifies the intentions and work of the band of philosophes in France. Originally intended as a simple revision and translation of Chambers's English *Cyclopedia*, Diderot determined to make of his *Encyclopedia* a new synthesis of human knowledge embodying the spirit of the Age of Reason. The distinguished mathematician D'Alembert wrote the famous preliminary essay; Voltaire, Montesquieu, Holbach, Buffon, and Rousseau among many others contributed articles. The seventeen folio volumes appearing between 1751 and 1765 were quickly followed by eleven volumes of plates and seven supplementary volumes. Twice interrupted by governmental suppression and impeded by endless difficulties, both financial and editorial, the *Encyclopedia* proved to be a magnificent triumph for Diderot and stands as one of the glories of the Enlightenment. Some of the material was routine, some was adapted from earlier compilations. Instead of the objectivity sought in modern works of this kind, the *Encyclopedia* was a crusading enterprise. Superstition and intolerance were attacked, along with royal absolutism and even the very concept of kingship. Strong emphasis was given to the role of science and to the creeds of humanitarianism and progress. Perhaps most striking was the emphasis upon technology. (Diderot's father was a skilled craftsman, a maker of surgical instruments.) This was true of the articles and also of the superb illustrations, where every detail of manufacture and craftsmanship was depicted in plates that were both handsomely produced and meticulously detailed. Nothing could have better expressed the empirical, experimental atmosphere of the age. The influence of the *Encyclopedia* can hardly be doubted. The original edition had forty-three hundred subscribers, following which six further editions were issued before the end of the century.

Possibly the greatest name of this period and certainly the most difficult to classify as a philosophe was Jean Jacques Rousseau. The son of a

Genevan watchmaker, an "original" with little formal education, a social misfit who drifted through life living with an illiterate servant girl each of whose five children was regularly turned over to an orphanage, he was never at home in a society that sought to lionize him and never truly at home with himself. His genius was to be able to write profoundly on great issues and with a perfectly adapted prose style. His *New Héloise* was a major landmark in the emergence of the preromantic novel; his *Emile*, the most original educational work of the eighteenth century, depicted the child who had been brought up in perfect naturalness to grow, to unfold from within, to feel, and to be. The *Emile* has been hailed as the Charter of Childhood, and in some circles has been equally strongly condemned. His *Confessions* remain as one of the great documents revealing the complexities of a tormented human soul.

Rousseau's political writings give him his eminent place in the history of the Enlightenment. His first early prize winning *Discourse on the Arts and Sciences* (1750) brought him to attention because of the provocative thesis that the progress of the arts and the sciences has destroyed the virtues of an earlier natural state of mankind and has contributed to the moral corruption of man. His subsequent *Discourse on the Origins of Inequality* (1754) held that the first man to fence a piece of common land was the true creator of private property and the originator of the glaring inequalities of civil society. To some interpreters this has marked Rousseau as a pioneer in the history of modern socialism; to others he was not the enemy of all existing society—he was the enemy of a society so organized as to prevent men from realizing their true selves.

The purpose of Rousseau's *Social Contract*, published in 1762, was to find a "sure and legitimate rule" for civil society, "men being taken as they are and laws as they might be." "Man is born free," Rousseau wrote, meaning presumably that man is born for freedom, "and everywhere he is in chains." The chains are the bonds which have been put upon him by civil society. Rousseau's purpose was to show that the chains of civil society can be considered legitimate if we understand the way in which the state comes into being, and if we can discover and apply the true principles of its organization. Rousseau began with the assumption of a prior state of nature from which men had emerged by means of a social contract. This involved no surrender to a sovereign whose only authority depended upon force. "Each, while uniting himself with all, may still obey only himself and remain as free as before." The agreement is a "*social* contract" binding the members to one another. "Each, giving himself to all, gives himself to none." Men put themselves "under the supreme direction of the general will," which is their own. The people, therefore, always are (or always should be) sovereign.

Beneath the difficulties and subtleties of Rousseau's thought are to be found ideas fundamental to the modern conception of a democratic society. He had no illusions about the problem of their application in his own age. At one point in the *Social Contract* he wrote: "Were there a people of gods, their government would be democratic. So perfect a government is not for men." Possibly the best chance for democracy would be in the small cantons of Switzerland. For a country as large as France monarchy would seem unavoidable, but it should be a monarchy very different from what then existed. As for England, Rousseau observed that the people there were free only during the election of members of Parliament.

Despite the great success of Rousseau's other works, the *Social Contract* had no immediate dramatic impact; it sold poorly, and a second edition was not printed until twenty years later. The cautious and moderate leaders of the American Revolution gave less welcome to Rousseau than they did to Locke and Montesquieu, nor did he come into his own in France until the first stages of the French Revolution were over. Then a statue of Rousseau was placed in the meeting place of the Convention, and with the rise of Robespierre—a reader of Rousseau since his youth—he may be said to have triumphed.

The influence exerted not only by Rousseau but by the entire generation of philosophes upon the actual course of events in France has been variously interpreted. The historian Taine contended that the philosophes poisoned the minds of their generation and created a revolutionary atmosphere which not even the presence of great abuses, acknowledged by Taine, could justify. Students nowadays find the explanation of the crises of 1788 and 1789 in a very broad range of forces going far beyond the printed word. The first daily paper of the capital, the *Journal de Paris*, did not appear until 1779. Daniel Mornet has examined the figures for the sale of various types of books in the period preceding the French Revolution and has shown that, as might be expected, the works of the philosophes did not constitute anything like a major part. It would be inconceivable, moreover, that there could be a general impact upon a public largely unable to read. A sampling of parish registers at the close of the *ancien régime* has shown that over half the men and nearly three-quarters of the women could not even sign their names to the marriage registers. With the exception of Condorcet not one of the major philosophes lived to see the French Revolution. What their generation had done was to formulate an impressive range of new critical ideas and to preach them so persuasively that they had become the common possession of the solid men who for the most part made up the Constituent Assembly of 1789.

2

FROM REFORM
TO REVOLUTION
1774–1789

The Revolutionary Problem

Today's world which is so full of revolutionary crises can still look back to the French Revolution as the great initiator of modern nineteenth-century European political systems. What was its nature? Certainly it was much more than the bloody melodrama described by Charles Dickens and Thomas Carlyle. The years of the Revolution with their Napoleonic sequel can be regarded as the most dramatic, and in many ways the most significant, segment of all French history. French political leaders and parties have ever since refought its battles. Lord Acton described the Revolution in a memorable phrase as the great turning point of modern history. A turning point it undoubtedly was in the history of Europe as well as in the history of France, though Acton wrote too early to be aware of the enormous revolutionary upheavals of our own day—revolutions on a scale vaster than was that which had occurred in France. Even so, the enormous impact of the Revolution on the land of its birth was undeniable. On one side of the Revolution lay the privileged, monarchical, quasi-feudal society of the *ancien régime;* on the other side lay the parliamentary, bourgeois, semiindustrialized, potentially democratic world of the nineteenth century. Few contrasts could be more striking.

Most historical phenomena can be at least partially understood in terms of their origins. Simplistic explanations of the origins of the French Revolution have been both numerous and contradictory. It was, so some

23

have held, the legitimate uprising of the people against the intolerable tyranny of their masters. To others it was the concrete embodiment of the dreams of the philosophes—those crusaders of the salon and the printed page whose essentially revolutionary ideas led men of action to create a more rational, a more humane, and a more just world. To still others it was the outcome of the sinister conspiracy of wicked men, bent on destroying a regime whose generally admitted defects could better have been met by the gradual process of reform. The Revolution has also been widely interpreted as a class movement which brought the bourgeoisie, steadily growing in education and economic prosperity, into control of the state, thereby achieving a social position which had long been denied them. A variant of such socioeconomic interpretations would lay great stress on the role of the peasant. Since the enormous preponderance of Frenchmen were tillers of the soil and since most of the land of France was encumbered with burdensome survivals from a feudal past, the mounting resentment at such conditions, so it is held, led eventually to an explosion. A further development in the study of the French Revolution has been the painstaking investigation of the nature of the crowds which on the many critical "days" of the Revolution took violent action in the streets. Such investigations also take into account the particular types of grievances—largely concerning wages and the prices of food—with which these crowds were concerned. It is reasonably clear that the little people (*menu peuple*) or, as they came to be known, the *sans-culottes*, were not a rabble from the gutter but were predominantly artisans, shopkeepers, employees of various types, and in general members of the petty bourgeoisie. Such people played a much larger role as the Revolution progressed. They were in no position at an earlier time even to make their grievances heard. Yet the fact of their discontent cannot be doubted, and thus one must include this resentment along with that of the much larger class of country dwellers in understanding the developing crisis of the *ancien régime*.

Still another explanation would stress the administrative crisis in France. A governmental system which had worked reasonably well under the driving force of Louis XIV became impossible under his two successors. Inefficiently centralized, corrupt, and highly privileged, this system defied the efforts of able ministers to reform it. The financial crisis in particular became so grave that reform of some sort clearly was inescapable. Yet reform attempted from above immediately encountered the opposition of vested interests, particularly of certain privileged bodies of officials: the Parlement of Paris, the provincial parlements, and the provincial estates. The administrative nobility dominating these assemblies and locked in struggle with the régime at last urged the summoning of the Estates General of the realm to authorize measures which would meet the crisis. Royal assent to this proposal meant the opening of the floodgates.

Some scholars have tried to put the French Revolution in a much broader perspective, seeing it as part of a widespread secular unrest growing up on both sides of the Atlantic—an unrest directed against the general power of aristocracies exercising their authority through "constituted bodies." Such is the underlying theme of what Jacques Godechot has called the Atlantic Revolution, and Robert Palmer has called the Age of the Democratic Revolution.[1]

It would seem wise to agree simply that the Revolution was a most complex phenomenon; that no single cause will fully explain it; that it began as an effort to solve an administrative and financial crisis, in the course of which it revealed the deep currents of unrest running through the *ancien régime;* and that it resulted in substantial changes in the political, social, and economic fabric of France. The violence of the Revolution now appears moderate in terms of what one has been obliged to face today, and in any case this violence was largely unpremeditated. Few expected the Revolution to follow the course which actually it did; and in its background, its development, and its legacies it reached out far beyond France itself. It was, in the words of a recent writer, "The First European Revolution." [2]

The Crisis in Government

A generation ago Louis Madelin entitled his account of the reign of Louis XVI and Marie Antoinette "The Twilight of the Monarchy," a touchingly appropriate phrase in relation to the fate of the doomed couple. Yet the reign which opened in 1774 did not seem necessarily fated to meet disaster. Though poorly trained by his grandfather for the duties of kingship, and lacking completely in those qualities that had marked Henry IV and Louis XIV, the new king was well intentioned. The young Marie Antoinette, sent from Vienna by her mother, Maria Theresa, to cement the understanding between Austria and France, was frivolous, light-headed, and wildly extravagant. It did not embarrass her, for example, to lose in one evening at cards the equivalent of a hundred thousand dollars, and she was equally extravagant in her generosity to her friends.

[1] See Godechot's *La Grande nation* (2 vols. Paris, 1956), and Palmer's *Age of the Democratic Revolution* (2 vols. Princeton, 1959, 1964).
[2] Norman Hampson, *The First European Revolution: 1776–1815* (1969).

ADMINISTRATIVE DIVISIONS IN FRANCE BY 1789

The varying size of the forty provinces arose from the differences in their feudal origin. The thirty-three *généralités*, each the responsibility of an intendant, corresponded roughly to the provinces. The map shows that the provincial estates had developed in the outlying provinces. By 1789 these estates were functioning only at Rennes, Dijon, Toulouse, Pau, Aix-en-Provence, and Grenoble.

Monarchy had always provided leadership in France. From the days of the Capetians the king had stood at the center of the administrative machine. The Estates General—that body, medieval in origin, which spoke for the three estates of the realm—had not been summoned since 1614. No cabinet existed in the English sense and, although Louis XVI certainly was not lacking in experienced and able advisors, he had no *premier ministre* in the great tradition of Sully, Richelieu, Mazarin, or Fleury. The king was advised by a series of councils over which he theoretically presided—functional divisions of the *Conseil du Roi* whose origins went back to the Middle Ages. Decrees emanating from these bodies became the law of the land, though the Parlement of Paris, which had the duty of enregistering these decrees, had at least a delaying power over them. The several provincial parlements had some similar local duty to enregister and supervise the enforcement of royal ordinances. By 1774 the technical operation of government was directed by seven ministers: the chancellor, the keeper of the seals, the controller general of finances, and the four secretaries of state for foreign affairs, war, marine, and the royal household. These men were not automatically members of the Royal Council, they did not meet as a group, and they were essentially agents and servants of the king. Very significantly, the most prominent ministerial position was that of controller general of finances.

One enormous difficulty of the French government lay in the effort to impose its authority from Paris or Versailles upon the provinces. No genuinely uniform system of administration had been devised for a France which like all European countries had experienced a slow growth from a decentralized feudal régime to one of more or less efficiently organized royal authority. Even the term *province* was confusing. Medieval France had been made up of a mass of feudal principalities over which royal authority had slowly been extended. In the eighteenth century the forty *gouvernements*, each having a royal governor whose original duties had been largely military, corresponded roughly to the historic units of an older France. Under a different scheme of arrangement which did not tally precisely with the provincial boundaries, France was also divided into thirty-four *généralités*, each of these marking the sphere of authority of an intendant—the agent sent from Paris to see that the royal will was carried out. (See map, p. 26)

Provincial estates had existed in some nine or ten frontier provinces known as the *pays d'états*. These relics of feudalism were local representative assemblies which were in no sense democratic and had been allowed to continue when such outlying lands became a part of the French Kingdom. By the reign of Louis XVI provincial estates were functioning only in Brittany, Burgundy, and in the southern areas which comprised Béarn,

Languedoc, and Provence. These assemblies, speaking chiefly in the name of the local aristocratic landholders, did give some scope to local initiative, especially in fiscal matters, and acted as some check on the royal intendants.

Another institution capable of obstructing the operation of the royal government was that of the parlements. These were legal bodies of great antiquity whose basic duty was to review the decisions of lower courts. The Parlement of Paris was the greatest, with a full membership of about two hundred. The members, rich magistrates usually with the status of nobility (*noblesse de robe*), had acquired their offices by purchase from the state and could pass them on to their heirs by means of an appropriate payment. The Parlement of Paris had among its duties the responsibility of entering royal edicts and ordinances upon its rolls.[3] Over the centuries it had developed the right of remonstrance, that is to say, of refusal to enregister an edict which seemed to be in conflict either with previous royal legislation or with what were taken to be the fundamental laws of the monarchy. Although the king could overrule such a remonstrance in a solemn ceremony known as a *lit de justice* (literally, a "Bed of Justice") and could further punish an obstreperous parlement by ordering its exile from the capital, the obstructive power of the body was clear. In addition to the great Parlement of Paris, twelve provincial bodies existed with similar, though obviously lesser, powers of judicial activity and at times of vigorous opposition.[4]

This complex administrative machine had both strengths and weaknesses. Though it had worked effectively under the strong driving hand of a Richelieu or a Louis XIV, it faltered badly under Louis XV and Louis XVI. The various ministries had developed a high degree of technical skill, and some of the intendants, for example, Turgot in Limoges, had been able to stimulate genuine local improvements. Both the provincial estates and the provincial parlements, even though their membership was largely privileged and aristocratic, provided at least some outlet for local grievances, as will be clear in the crisis of 1788. Perhaps the greatest governmental weakness lay in the lack of order and consistency. Nowhere was this truer than in the fields of justice and finance. The southern half of France, was the land of a written law derived from Rome; the northern half was administered under the customary law arising from the unwritten usages of the early Frankish tribes. Justice, such as it was, was enforced

---

[3] See J. H. Shennan, *The Parlement of Paris* (1968).
[4] These local parlements, with dates of foundation, were: Toulouse (1443), Grenoble (1453), Bordeaux (1472), Dijon (1477), Aix-en-Provence (1501), Rouen (1515), Rennes (1554), Pau (1620), Metz (1633), Besançon (1676), Douai (1700), Nancy (1776).

in a chaotic series of royal, manorial, and ecclesiastical courts. Thus, though the overall historic tendency of government had been in the direction of centralization, its actual operation was scandalously inefficient. What that perspicacious observer Alexis de Tocqueville characterized as "a strict rule, a loose enforcement," was essentially true.

If the actual machinery of government was weak, the specific matter of finances produced immediate and appalling difficulties. In a country operating without a budget the public knew at least this much about its affairs: that annual deficits grew steadily larger. Price rises, a standard phenomenon of the eighteenth century, and the large role assumed by the central government accounted for a part of such deficits. The major reason lay, however, in the heavy cost of the four wars in which France had engaged in the half-century from 1733 to 1783. Not only were these costs heavy, but they were met increasingly by borrowing at interest rates which varied from 8½ to 10 percent. The government fell steadily behind in its obligations, borrowing new money not to reduce the capital amount of its debts but simply to meet the most urgent interest payments. In essence, therefore, the government chose to put off the evil day rather than meet its obligations. In the very last year of the *ancien régime*, when an attempt was made to clarify the picture of governmental expenses, the startling figures which emerged can be summarized as follows:

ESTIMATES FOR 1788

Interest charges on the public debt	318,000,000 livres	(51%)
Defense and diplomatic services	165,500,000 "	(26%)
All civil expenditures	146,000,000 "	(23%)
	629,500,000	(100%)

Equally significant was the outrageous way in which taxes were imposed and collected.[5] The direct taxes, principally the *taille, capitation,* and *vingtième,* were subject to mounting protest. The *corvée* bore particularly unfairly on the peasants, who resented having to labor upon the roads for the benefit of merchants and other travelers who passed over them. A similar and growing resentment was felt at the burden of the indirect taxes, chiefly customs duties and excises. Peasants also were subject to a tithe, or annual payment in produce to the Church, originally set at one-tenth of the crops, but in fact generally less. The most hated impositions were the dues owed to the lord of the manor, both personal and monetary, surviving from medieval times and still encumbering the

[5] For earlier periods see E. J. Knapton, *France* (1971), pp. 112, 142, 212.

soil of France. Usually these dues continued to be exacted even after the peasant had become the supposed owner of his land. In addition to payments in money and produce, customary usage required the peasant to use his lord's mill or bakeoven and to be subject for petty offenses to fines imposed in the manorial courts. Still other outrageous burdens were the *capitaineries*, or hunting rights, guaranteeing the lord the rights of the chase even over newly planted fields and forbidding the farmer to drive off game which was destroying his crops. What made the financial system seem outrageous to a growing number of Frenchmen was not simply the steady march towards governmental bankruptcy in what was essentially a thriving country. The evidence grew on every hand that taxes were most unfairly levied, most inefficiently collected, and most extravagantly and unreasonably spent.

The Conflict of Class Interests

The simple fact of vast social inequality was apparent in France, as indeed it was everywhere in Europe. The agrarian problem loomed very large, for out of a French population estimated in 1789 at twenty-six millions, some twenty-two millions lived on the soil. Their status varied greatly. Some were quite well-to-do, so that the word *paysan* is better translated "country dweller" than simply "peasant." Only about a million Frenchmen were still serfs, and these were largely in the newly acquired eastern frontier provinces. About five millions were landless day laborers. The largest group were *métayers*, a term loosely translated as "sharecroppers," farming a piece of land and turning over perhaps half the crop to the landlord. These, along with peasants owning small portions of land and farming other areas by dependent tenures, would number about fifteen millions. Those peasants who owned their land free of major encumbrances have been estimated to number about a million.

The surface of rural France with its fine new royal roads, which by 1789 extended to a total of twenty-five thousand miles, its vineyards, olive groves, grainfields, and orchards was of a complexity that defies simple generalization. The English agriculturalist Arthur Young, whose *Travels in France* described the countryside in the years 1787, 1788, and 1789, gave a mixed picture of comfortable prosperity alternating with extreme poverty. The real and crushing burden for the peasant was that of taxes, yet the steady upward price rise of the eighteenth century also affected him as it did everyone else. A recurrence of poor harvests more than once reached the proportions of famine, notably in 1725,

1740, 1759, 1766–1768, and 1772–1776. A marked feature was the increasing number of brigands and beggars. General price rises have been calculated as amounting to between 50 and 60 percent, in a period when average wages had risen by only 22 percent. Moreover, between the years 1776 and 1787 and within the general long-term upward movement of prices an actual decline took place in the prices farmers received for their products. Thus, despite some outward appearance of prosperity, the peasant problem had risen to major proportions and began to have a substantial impact upon French social thought.

The coming of a revolutionary crisis has sometimes been attributed to a growing sense of social injustice in the urban centers, sparked by the new ideas of the philosophes. It is clear that the philosophes had again and again directed their shafts against the inequities of society and against the system of privilege which marked the *ancien régime*. In Beaumarchais's play *The Marriage of Figaro* the hero, a traveling barber, denounces his rival, a count, in a famous soliloquy:

> No, Monsieur le Comte, you shan't have her! You shan't
> have her. Because you are a great noble, you think you are
> a great genius! Nobility, a fortune, a rank, appointments to
> office: all this makes a man so proud! What did you do to
> earn all this? You took the trouble to be born—nothing
> more.

This passage had a wildly enthusiastic welcome when the play was first produced at Paris in 1784. Such a response was indicative no doubt of a growing willingness to level criticisms at the system of social privilege from which only a few drew substantial advantages.

The court, with its empty-headed extravagances, was clearly separated from the day-to-day life of France. The realm was divided into three estates, or orders of people; two of them, though only a tiny fraction of the total, had enormous privileges. The First Estate, the clergy, numbering something less than 150,000, held great landed wealth, possibly 15 percent of the cultivable soil of France. It also had the large revenues coming from the tithe which it imposed upon all farm and dairy produce. Marked divergences existed within the privileged ranks of the clergy. The prince-archbishop of Strasbourg had an annual income of 400,000 livres; the obscure bishop of Vence had to be satisfied with 7,000 livres. Nomination to bishoprics and abbacies was in the hands of the king; and in 1789 every one of the French bishops and archbishops was of noble birth. Exempt from regular taxation, the general assembly of the clergy professed to meet its obligations by regularly voting "free gifts" to the state. Yet it is important to notice that while the higher clergy were in general privileged and worldly and became a popular subject for attack by the philosophes, the lower clergy tended to come from a different level of society. Many parish priests were the sons of peasants, with little hope of rising within the framework of the Church; thus they tended to sympathize with the grievances of their flocks and in due course to accept the Revolution.

The nobility of France presented a very complex picture. One can estimate their number at about 400,000, among them the princely nobility of blood, the traditional country nobility of the sword, and the new administrative nobility of the robe. Another type of noble was the *hobereau*, often living in a broken-down manor house and seeming little different in externals from his peasant neighbors or tenants. Yet somewhere he possessed a faded patent of nobility, he asserted his right to have a bell tower and a dovecote and to hunt over the manorial fields; aware that he was entitled to money and personal services from his tenants, he strained every effort to exact them and in some cases even to enlarge them.

The eighteenth century was a great age for the French aristocracy. They owned perhaps one-fifth of the cultivable soil of France; by virtue of their ancient role as protector of the peasant they could exercise their seigneurial rights to personal services and money payments from the nonnoble class of landholders. They were securely entrenched in public service. They lived delightfully and most elegantly in their country châteaux and in their graceful town *hôtels*. A patent of 1781 required that any candidate for an army commission should have all four grandparents of noble birth. Undeniably many of the nobles, in a deeper sense than mere dilettantism, were interested in the ideas of the philosophes; some of them—Talleyrand, Mirabeau, La Rochefoucauld, and Condorcet, for example—were to accept the Revolution. Yet as a class they were, along with the clergy, the embodiment of a system of privilege that clearly had outlived its usefulness.

The Third Estate comprised everyone who was neither noble nor clerical. This class would constitute at least 98 percent of the French population. Town dwellers alone would account for about 2,000,000, Paris being now estimated to have some 650,000 inhabitants; Lyon had 135,000; Marseille, 90,000; Bordeaux, 76,000; and Rouen, 72,000. One has to visualize among them a spectrum of occupations extending from the professional group of lawyers, doctors, and the like, through prosperous merchants, bankers, and industrialists, skilled craftsmen, petty shopkeepers, and domestic servants, to what could be called the beginnings of a true urban proletariat. A considerable degree of "enlightenment" had spread among the upper groups of this bourgeoisie. These, along with a similarly enlightened group of noblemen, were to dominate the first stage of the French Revolution. The tendency to single out the relatively prosperous bourgeoisie, heavily burdened with taxes and denied social privileges and political power, as the true driving force of the French Revolution has been qualified somewhat by the realization, as has been earlier remarked, that noble landowners, too, were not as free from taxation as was once held. The lower ranks of the bourgeoisie are now known to have made up the largest part of the crowds that surged through the streets of Paris and other cities on the great "days" of the Revolution.

By far the largest component of the Third Estate was the peasantry. It is now estimated that about 35 percent of the cultivable soil of France was in peasant hands.[6] The heavy burdens imposed upon this class have already been indicated: direct and indirect royal taxes, clerical tithes, and seigneurial dues. In addition there were the burdens of recurrent crop failures, periodic near-famine conditions, and a century-long rise in prices which consistently outran increases in real wages. In the eighteenth century agrarian unrest could hardly start a revolution, and it is clear that conditions in rural France were far better than they were in central and eastern Europe. Yet this unrest could predictably contribute heavily to the course of revolution once it had begun.

The Last Reform Plans
of the *Ancien Régime*

At the very outset of the reign of Louis XVI his ministers were faced with the urgent necessity of reform. Louis first relied upon Jacques Turgot, a Physiocratic writer and experienced intendant who had had great success in the province of Limoges. As controller general of finances Turgot quickly launched a whole series of reforms intended to bring about some kind of financial and governmental order: economies in administration, free trade in grain, suppression of compulsory work on the roads, the abolition of the urban gilds on the ground that they were interfering with freedom of enterprise, and the establishment of a discount bank to aid the government with loans in times of crises. But Louis XVI unwisely had re-

---

[6] Miss C. B. A. Behrens, who has made technical studies of this subject, gives the following estimates for the ownership or holding of cultivated land in France by 1789: peasants, 35%; bourgeois investors, 30%; nobility, 20%; clergy, 15%. *The Ancien Régime* (1967), p. 38.

summoned the Parlement of Paris and the provincial parlements which had been dismissed in 1771 by his predecessor. These bodies were dominated by members of the privileged classes who feared the effect of possible reforms upon their special interests. Their influence, channeled in part through Queen Marie Antoinette, led Louis after two years to dismiss his capable minister, and with his fall in 1776 went any immediate hope for the success of his reforms. "I shall never," Voltaire wrote, "console myself for having seen rise and perish the golden age which these two ministers [Turgot and Malesherbes] were preparing for us."

For five years Jacques Necker, a Genevan financier and Protestant most notable to many as the father of Madame de Staël, held the post previously occupied by Turgot. Though he was an expert financier he was not truly a statesman. It made sense, to be sure, to seek economies in expenditure, to try to simplify administrative machinery, and to reduce the *taille* and the *gabelle*. Yet the war in support of Britain's American colonies to which France became committed, the restoration of the old gild system and the *corvée*, along with the heavy use of borrowing in order to keep the government solvent were basically unstatesmanlike. Necker has been praised for his *Compte rendu*, or financial statement, of 1781 in which he claimed to be giving the public a clear picture of what was happening both to income and expenditures. But many of the figures were deceptive; there was still no true budget; and though over a hundred thousand copies of the *Compte rendu* were quickly sold, the public was not truly mobilized in his support. Instead, those courtiers whom his reforms would have injured organized against him and in 1781 forced his resignation.

After two confused years another figure, the experienced intendant, Calonne, was appointed controller general of finances. Calonne's native abilities were substantial and he was quick to see that financial reforms and administrative reorganization were the two keys to the solution of the country's mounting difficulties. The annual deficits which Turgot and Necker had reduced were again increasing rapidly, so that government borrowing was becoming more difficult.[7] After considerable delay Calonne finally submitted to the king in August 1786 outlines of a comprehensive reform scheme. It is a striking indication of the ability still to be found under the *ancien régime* that Calonne's proposals anticipated

---

[7] Annual deficits were as follows: 1768— 70 m. livres
                                         1776— 37 m.   "
                                         1783— 80 m.   "
                                         1787—112 m.   "
The amount of short-term loans to the government, due to be repaid in the decade 1789–1799, amounted to 400 million livres.

much of what the moderate revolution later was to bring about. In the financial realm, Calonne proposed a reduction of 20 million livres annually in governmental expenditure. He would repay the short-term debt over a twenty-year, instead of a ten-year, period. A new stamp tax on documents would bring in further revenue, as would a direct tax on all landowners proportional to income, to replace the poll tax and the *vingtième*. This tax would be paid in crops, not in money. Several proposals sought to revitalize the economy. All internal customs barriers would be abolished and some indirect taxes (e.g., on tobacco) would be reduced. Something approaching free trade in grain was proposed. The burden of the most deeply resented taxes, *taille, gabelle,* and *corvée,* was also to be lessened.

Equally as significant as the financial reforms was the new machinery contemplated in order to carry them out. In those large portions of France where provincial estates did not exist, a pyramidal scheme of consultative assemblies was proposed. Each village of over a thousand inhabitants would have a parish assembly of rural proprietors for various local tasks. District assemblies would apportion royal taxes among towns and villages. At a third level there would be new provincial assemblies resembling those already existing in the *pays d'état* and having largely advisory duties. Calonne would make no distinction between the separate orders in these new bodies, and he would have them closely supervised by the existing royal agents, the intendants. In essence, therefore, he contemplated an efficient centralization, based essentially upon royal power, to replace the increasingly inefficient authority of the Bourbons. It seems correct to say that Calonne was seeking to place his country among the truly enlightened despotisms of the eighteenth century. In the nature of the opposition which arose to Calonne's plans and in the failure of his program can be found an important clue to the coming of the French Revolution. The phrase generally ascribed to this opposition is "the revolt of the nobles."

The Revolt of the Nobles

The distinguished historian Georges Lefebvre has remarked that the history of the Capetian monarchy was largely the story of its struggle against the aristocracy, and that the beginnings of the French Revolution were marked by "the last offensive of the aristocracy." This is the phenomenon associated with Calonne's reform proposals of 1786. Calonne was sure that if his plans were submitted to the Parlement of Paris they would immediately encounter the opposition of the vested interests represented there. He was not prepared to summon the Estates General of the realm, moribund since 1614. He therefore recommended instead that his plan be submitted to an assembly of notables. This was a kind of ad hoc body to be nominated by the king and composed of distinguished individuals, overwhelmingly aristocratic, drawn from various branches of public service. When it materialized, the total membership was 144, and of these fewer than 30 belonged to the Third Estate. When the notables actually did meet in February 1787, Calonne announced a deficit of eighty million livres which after a fire of questions he conceded would prove even larger. The opposition to Calonne's proposals was so violent and so varied that in April, aware of strong antagonism at the court, he resigned, withdrew to his estates in Lorraine, and soon after went into exile in England.

To replace Calonne, Louis XVI now made the unhappy choice of Loménie de Brienne, archbishop of Toulouse and one of the notables who had most vigorously opposed Calonne. Lefebvre calls him "an incompetent ignoramus." Brienne immediately ran into trouble with the notables. He promised economies in order to placate his critics, but he was compelled in the end to take up those financial proposals of Calonne which he had recently opposed. The notables then informed him that only the Estates General could assent to new taxes. The opposition to Brienne was so strong that in May 1787, Louis dissolved the notables. This was less a victory for the king than it was for the aristocracy, whose spokesmen had resoundingly defeated the plans for reform and who envisaged the Estates General as a body capable of protecting their special interests.

The next step was for the government to turn to the Parlement of Paris and the provincial parlements. The former approved some of Brienne's measures, which were a slightly modified version of those of Calonne. But it refused approval to the proposed new stamp tax and the tax on land, saying that only the Estates General could give this. Consequently, in August Louis XVI, meeting opposition when he held a *lit de justice*, exiled the Parlement of Paris to Troyes. This led to widespread public denunciation of the government. When the Parlement of Paris was recalled a month later, it immediately renewed its opposition, causing bitter conflict both with Louis and with Brienne. The struggle dragged on into 1788. Among other matters, the Parlement declared that *lettres de cachet* were contrary both to public law and to natural law. In May it issued a striking Declaration of Fundamental Laws. This stated in essence that monarchy was hereditary; that the nation, through the Estates General, had the right to consent freely to taxation; that the customs of the various French provinces were inviolable; that all Frenchmen had the right to be tried by irremovable judges; and that *lettres de cachet* should be abolished. This document was less an assertion of basic rights for all men than it was a clever invocation of such rights by a privileged group to protect its special interests. Louis struck back by arresting two leaders of the Parlement and by enforcing the registration of six royal edicts in a *lit de justice*. The effect of these edicts would have been to restrict the judicial power and destroy the political power of the thirteen parlements by creating a new Plenary Court.

The most striking consequence of this conflict was the spread of opposition in the provinces. Here the provincial parlements were made up of administrative officers—*noblesse de robe* and upper bourgeoisie—many of whom were familiar with the new intellectual ideas of the eighteenth century. Not the least important of the new attitudes was a widespread admiration for the parliamentary monarchy of Great Britain. The repeated demands for the summoning of the Estates General suggested the hope that France might move in this direction. The opposition in the provinces and the airing of such demands created an atmosphere of revolt in some parts of France a year before the Revolution in the conventional sense had broken out.

The large area over which disturbances occurred was significant. Usually the provincial parlement, seeing its powers taken from it by the monarchy, became the center of protest. This was true in the South—in Provence, Dauphiné, at Toulouse and at Bordeaux. There were also disturbances in Brittany, in Burgundy, and in Hainaut. Food shortages and high prices made it easy for local officers to stimulate popular unrest. The widespread demand now being heard was to summon the Estates General, the one historic body of proportions adequate to cope with the threat of national bankruptcy. At Grenoble in June 1788 crowds assembled when the parlement of Dauphiné, having protested against some royal edicts, was ordered into exile. Peasants joined with members of the local craft gilds to attack representatives of the king at the town hall. In the end the commandant capitulated and the magistrates of the parlement reassembled. In July the provincial estates of the Dauphiné reconstituted themselves at Vizille, not far from Grenoble, in the château of a wealthy merchant. The striking fact in the composition of this assembly is that the clergy numbered 60, the nobles numbered 165, and the delegates from the various municipalities numbered about 500. For the first time, therefore, the Third Estate dominated an assembly. This formally declared itself ready to abandon its local privileges if the Dauphiné could participate in a truly national assembly, that is, the Estates General. A local tablet claims with some justice that here in July 1788 the Revolution began.

The crisis ended when Brienne agreed on July 5, 1788, to summon the Estates General. The date of meeting was set soon after for May 1, 1789. When Brienne resigned late in August the king reappointed Necker as his principal advisor. Soon afterwards the Parlement of Paris was recalled. The essence of this confused year was that the aristocracy, as Lefebvre said, had formed a common front against royal power. It had done this in the defense of its own interests; yet it had made genuine reform, if not as yet revolution, inevitable. An important feature of the Estates General soon to be elected and soon to undertake the great transformation of France is that it was dominated by men both noble and bourgeois in origin who had taken a large part in the protests, debates, moves, and countermoves of 1787 and 1788. Hardly a one would have considered himself a revolutionary.

3

THE MODERATE
REVOLUTION
1789–1792

From Estates General to Constituent Assembly

The chain of events leading France inexorably from reform to revolution was forged in 1788. When Necker was recalled to succeed Brienne, his problems were enormous. His great skill as a financier was hardly evident in the baffling world of politics, for he had no large plans for administrative reforms and little sense that France was on the threshold of a new age.

If the Estates General were to be summoned as they had been in 1614 with each order—Clergy, Nobility, Third Estate—sitting separately and having equal representation, the old class structure of French society would be perpetuated. The privileged groups who had resisted the reform proposals of Turgot, Calonne, and Brienne assumed that the Estates General so summoned would enable them to continue their successful opposition. On the other hand, a growing number of magistrates, enlightened nobles, some clergy, and some publicists had other views. Soon to be known as the patriotic party, though they were not in the modern sense truly a party, they wished an assembly that would champion a national rather than a class interest. They found their principal home in some Paris salons, in country châteaux such as that of the duke of Rochefoucauld, in a number of enlightened freemasonic lodges, in the coffeehouses of the Palais-Royal, and in many newly organized clubs and societies.

Along with their activities came a remarkable flood of pamphlet literature dramatizing the concept of France as a nation and insisting on the need for an actual constitution which would assert those rights inherent in all men and make definite the new machinery by which France should be governed. Easily the most famous example of such material was a pamphlet written by the abbé Sieyès, an enlightened canon of Chartres cathedral. Sieyès insisted in his *What Is the Third Estate?* that the Third Estate was not simply one of the three orders, but constituted in fact the nation. Hence the Third Estate should have membership at least equalling the combined total of the other two, and voting should not be by order but by head. In a decree of December 1788 ("A New Year's Gift for France"), Louis promised the Third Estate double representation but ignored the problem of vote by head. Nobility and clergy would choose representatives in their own provincial assemblies. For the choice of the Third Estate representatives all male taxpayers over twenty-five would vote locally for electors who subsequently would choose the deputies to go to Versailles. This meant that the choices would largely turn out to be men of experience—lawyers, municipal officers, and the like—and in some cases even clergy or nobles. Sieyès, for example, who was an abbé, sat with the Third Estate, as did Mirabeau, who was a marquis.

Each local electoral group had to prepare a formal statement (*cahier*) of its grievances, those of the Third Estate being first drafted locally (often on some model) and then sent to the secondary electoral bodies to be reduced to a single *cahier*. In them loyalty to the monarchy was repeatedly expressed, though there was much criticism of ministerial despotism and of the way in which individual liberties were ignored. France, it was widely held, should be given a defined constitutional structure. The great injustices of the legal and the tax systems should be remedied, and (at least so the Third Estate felt) the outworn system of manorial dues and services should be brought to an end. While some of the lower clergy managed to speak out against ecclesiastic privilege, in general the first two orders were careful to make a defense of their historic rights. One must, in summary, envisage in the *cahiers* a widespread demand for reform rather than any threat of impending violent revolution.

Although nearly two-thirds of the chosen members of the First Estate were parish priests and only about one-third were higher clergy, the general tone of this, as well as of the Second Estate, was conservative. The membership of the Third Estate was drawn largely from the professional classes—lawyers, judges, merchants, financiers, town officials, and the like. Among these groups the ideas of the Enlightenment had struck root. They might, therefore, be considered popular champions, even though the actual proletariat—a term to be sure not as yet in use—had no representation of its own. In general one is struck by the substantial, responsible nature of the members of the Third Estate, as one could also be impressed by the presence of a minority with similar views in the first two orders.

Financial reforms, urgently advocated by Louis XVI and Necker when the Estates General met at Versailles in May 1789 were momentarily put aside amid the growing demands for political equality. This, in the eyes of the Third Estate, would be impossible if the orders met and voted separately. When disagreement arose over the question of having the credentials of all deputies verified in common, the Third Estate, backed by a few clergy, voted by a large majority to call itself the National Assembly. A few days later, finding its usual meeting place locked, the Third Estate adjourned to the nearest large building, a tennis court. Here, amid intense excitement and again with some clerical support, those present took on June 20 the famous oath, "never to separate . . . until the constitution of the kingdom shall be laid and established upon secure foundations." Some nobles and a substantial group of the clergy soon associated themselves with what the Third Estate had done. At the close of a joint meeting on June 23, when the three orders were instructed by a royal representative to adjourn and meet separately, Mirabeau, speaking not so much for the Third Estate as for the nation, made his historic reply: "Go and tell those who sent you that we are here by will of the people, and will leave our places only if compelled by armed force." [1] Louis's typical capitulation, in which he instructed the clergy and nobles to meet with the others, was a historic landmark in the overthrow of the ancient system of privilege.

If the period preceding the meeting of the Estates General can be characterized as "the revolt of the nobles," the events just described mark the growing assertiveness of the great bourgeois interest. What followed was the injection of an element of violence which was more truly that of the common people. Violence, to be sure, had not been absent in the past. The "Flour War" (*Guerre des Farines*) of 1775 had seen riots in various parts of France as an explosive protest against the rising price of bread. By 1789 flour was at its highest price since 1715 and wages had remained far behind. A huge riot prompted by these conditions in one of the poor neighborhoods of Paris, the *Emeute Reveillon* of April 1789 (Reveillon was the owner of a large manufactory of painted wallpapers), had resulted in some three hundred deaths—one of the bloodiest episodes of the entire revolutionary period.

The historic assault of July 14 on the Bastille must be seen against such

---

[1] This is an approximation of his reply, the exact words of which have not been preserved.

a stormy background. At Versailles Louis had warmly welcomed some further regiments summoned to keep watch over the capital and had dismissed Necker. Crowds in Paris attacked the numerous gates where the hated taxes on incoming loads of flour were collected. An informally organized bourgeois militia, seeking arms, forced the weak and indecisive governor of the Invalides, which served both as a military hospital and an arms center, to turn over between thirty thousand and forty thousand muskets stored there. Powder had been easily obtained at the Hôtel de Ville. The crowds then sought further weapons and powder at the Bastille, a grim medieval fortress standing in a working class neighborhood and notorious as the place where political suspects were held under *lettres de cachet*. Heavy losses were inflicted upon the assailants—a total of ninety-eight being killed as against only two or three of the defenders. The commandant, who badly bungled his duties, was later murdered and decapitated when being taken to the Hôtel de Ville. The fall of the Bastille was not "a clap of thunder in a clear sky," for it followed closely the widespread unrest of the preceding year. Nor did it mark the arrival of the "rabble." Five-sixths of the 954 identified "Conquerors of the Bastille" (who later obtained medals and organized themselves for annual reunions and celebrations) were modest artisans and one-sixth of them were bourgeois.

The sequel was significant. The king recalled Necker and visited Paris, where he was presented with the new red-white-and-blue cockade.[2] Two of the most respected members of the National Assembly assumed new posts: Lafayette became commander of the National Guard, and Bailly, the royal astronomer, became mayor of Paris.

The violence symbolized by the attack on the Bastille showed itself in other ways. Near-famine conditions, poor wages, and high prices all contributed to widespread summer disturbances known as the "Great Fear" which swept over large parts of the countryside. Hayricks and manor houses were burned along with the manorial records. Many landlords or their agents were killed. The exaggerated reports of such disturbances had an immediate effect on the deputies at Versailles, who turned from the laborious work of constitution making to what seemed more urgent tasks. On the night of August 4, in an atmosphere combining near panic and genuine desire for reform, a landless nobleman the viscount of Noailles proposed that taxes should be paid by all proportionately to their incomes, that dues and servitudes owed by peasants should be abolished

---

[2] The cockade and the first genuinely national flag, the tricolor, were made by adding the historic red and blue colors of the city of Paris to the white banner of the Bourbons.

without compensation to their landlords, and that all other manorial dues payable in money or kind be redeemable for one lump sum. Other nobles rose to back Noailles's proposals, and in what has been called "a hurricane of wild generosity" the second and third articles were voted. Although many peasants were unable to free themselves from the web of money payments, the bitterly resented personal services and hunting rights were abolished outright and in this sense a new age began for France.

It was entirely in keeping with the new spirit of philosophy that some basic formulation of principles should go along with such concrete changes. Lafayette had discussed such a project with Thomas Jefferson, the American ambassador to France, as early as January 1789, and a copy of the draft which Lafayette later submitted has been found with Jefferson's annotations upon it. On August 27, 1789, the Assembly voted its Declaration of the Rights of Man, a landmark in French, and indeed in European, history. It has been called with much appropriateness the death certificate of the Old Regime and the birth certificate of the new. Its essential features can be seen in the following extracts:

> Men are born and remain free and equal in rights. . . .
> These rights are liberty, property, security, and resistance to oppression.
>
> The source of all sovereignty resides essentially in the nation. . . .
>
> Law is the expression of the general will; all citizens have the right to concur . . . in its formulation.
>
> No man may be accused, arrested, or detained except in cases determined by law. . . . No one is to be disquieted because of his opinions, even religious. . . . Every citizen may speak, write, and think freely. . . .
>
> Since property is a sacred and inviolable right, no one may be deprived thereof unless a legally established public necessity requires it.
>
> Any society in which . . . the separation of powers is not determined has no constitution.

This document, with its stress on equality of rights, the sanctity of property, and the supremacy of the general will, was clearly an inheritance coming out of the eighteenth century from the ideas of Locke, Montesquieu, and to some extent Rousseau.

Violence soon showed itself in still another form. Louis XVI had delayed his assent to some new constitutional articles, and both he and Marie Antoinette appeared hostile to reform when attending the royal banquet given to the officers of the newly arrived Flanders Regiment at Versailles. Such news, along with the continued flour shortages and high prices, led some popular journals at Paris to demand the transfer of the Assembly to the capital. Early in October a crowd of indignant housewives, along with some men disguised as such, marched the thirteen miles to Versailles and made their demands known to the Assembly. There is evidence that even some well-to-do ladies either marched or sent their servants to march for them. During the night a mob broke into the royal apartments, murdered some of the royal bodyguard, and narrowly missed killing the queen. Louis's characteristic choice again was to capitulate. He agreed to transfer his court to Paris, setting out in the morning amid a most unroyal procession of Paris housewives, National Guards, members of the Assembly, and hangers-on. He took up his residence at the Tuileries, while the Assembly soon found quarters in the *Manège*, the royal riding school nearby. With these moves a new phase of the Revolution had begun, for the influence of Paris would be greater now than ever before.

The Making of a New France, 1789–1791

After the fevered summer of 1789 what seemed to be a lull set in. The overall picture was that of the renamed National Constituent Assembly working for two years in relative harmony and ultimately producing an astonishing body of constructive legislation. This was destined to transform France and in large part to remain as a permanent legacy for the future.

Despite the general harmony, certain new trends contributed a note of uncertainty. The emigration of some nobles and clergy had begun as early as the time of the country disturbances in the summer of 1789. The number of such *émigrés* steadily increased and included even Louis XVI's two brothers, the count of Provence and the count of Artois. During the autumn of 1789 some 200,000 passports were issued, and in several Rhineland cities substantial bodies of Frenchmen began to congregate. Such people almost by definition were bitterly opposed to the changes occurring in France, though it was too early as yet for them to consider any specific way of bringing their opposition to bear. Time, however, was to make their opposition a concrete force working against the new order.

Another striking phenomenon was the growing activity of various new political clubs. The club, as its name implies, had been an importation from Georgian England. Some of the aristocratic groups represented a continuance of the salon tradition of the *ancien régime*. Others had a quite natural beginning in the association of deputies from a particular part of France, for example Brittany or the Gironde, seeking a convenient center at Versailles and later in Paris for meals, reading, and discussion. Still others were organized definitely to champion new and increasingly radical ideas, for example, the Society of the Friends of the Rights of Man which, moving into an abandoned convent of the order of the Cordeliers, soon took that originally religious name. The most famous of all such organizations, beginning as a group of Breton deputies at Versailles with the name Society of the Friends of the Constitution, established itself in a former Jacobin convent at Paris and under the new title of "Jacobins" became the most powerful club of the entire French Revolution. Such clubs were in essence arenas where issues could be debated by their members, plans developed, reputations made, and pressures of various sorts be applied to the National Assembly.

Still another phenomenon was the striking growth of the press. Literally hundreds of papers sprang up, covering the entire spectrum of opinions. Many were short-lived; many resembled pamphlets or newsletters more than they did the newspapers of today; and many spoke with increasing violence in what had come to be an entire absence of censorship. Without any question the journals of the left showed the most striking growth.

A decree of December 1789 had set up a new pattern of elected municipal government and of local militia units. Paris, a city of more than half a million, was divided into forty-eight sections, each with its local administration and its citizen militia. Here a newly recognized body of citizens found an important outlet for its opinions and was in time able to push the moderate program of reform into more radical channels.

The great reform measures passed piecemeal by the Assembly were by the autumn of 1791 finally embodied in two major documents, the Constitution of 1791 and the Civil Constitution of the Clergy. There were also further important steps in the field of finances. Rather than trace the laborious stages by which the work was done, it will be simpler to consider the completed product—the total, dramatic transformation of the political, and to some degree the social and economic, structure of France.

Politically, France became a limited monarchy. All titles of nobility and hereditary distinctions were abolished. All Frenchmen had the basic rights of citizenship, though not all had the vote. In May 1791 civil rights were specifically granted to free blacks. Legislative power was to be in the hands of a freely elected Legislative Assembly; supreme executive power was delegated by the nation to the monarchy whose title was fixed by primogeniture in the male line of the reigning family; judicial power was put in the hands of popularly elected judges. The legislature of 745 members was to be elected for two years by a system of indirect voting. To vote in the primary assemblies citizens had to be twenty-five years of age and pay an annual direct tax equal to three days' labor. An estimated 4,300,000 Frenchmen were given the vote in this way and some 3,000,000 were denied it. The electors chosen in the primary assemblies had to pay a direct tax equal to ten days of labor. The deputies whom they sent to Paris had to be owners of real estate and to pay an even more substantial tax. Despite all these limitations, since the legislature was to initiate and vote all laws, over which the king had no permanent veto, and since it fixed taxes, controlled expenditures, and made declarations of war, France had become more truly self-governing than any of its European neighbors, Great Britain not excepted.

Executive power was in the hands of the king, who took an oath to be faithful to the nation and the law. He appointed and dismissed his ministers, six in number, who had to countersign all royal orders. The king through his ministers had the power to propose declarations of war, appoint ambassadors, and conduct foreign affairs. It was ominous for the future that his genuine cooperation was essential for the practical working of the new regime.

A sweeping reorganization took place in the field of justice—the third branch of the division of powers. Some of the very early work of the Constituent Assembly was to sweep away the complex network of antiquated laws and to abolish torture, the pillory, public confession, and branding with hot irons. An entirely new system of courts, beginning with local justices of the peace and rising through district, departmental, and commercial tribunals to the Court of Cassation and the High Court at Paris was set up.[3] All judges were to be elected for a determined period of years, and juries were to be used in criminal cases. Historians have generally regarded this judicial work of the Constituent Assembly as among its best.

A major problem was to create an orderly system of local government

---

[3] The Court of Cassation could "break" (casser) the decision of a lower tribunal on the grounds of flaws in procedure alone. The High Court considered offenses committed by high public officials. There was no supreme court in the American sense.

throughout France to replace the baffling confusions of the *ancien régime*. The old provinces, or *généralités*, were swept away and in their place were set up eighty-three departments, roughly equal in size, and of such an extent that no place would be more than a day's journey from the chief town. Each department had an elected departmental council. For administrative purposes each was divided into districts and these in turn into cantons. At the base of the pyramid were the forty-four thousand *communes*, or municipalities, with their elected mayors and councils and their local units of the National Guard. Thus, at the grass roots level a democratic, communal pattern was established, in striking contrast to the authoritarian rule of the *ancien régime*. Here is to be found one of the great constructive works of the Revolution, for from that period to the present departmental and local governments have retained the essential characteristics then given to them.

More immediately important to the men of 1789 was the problem of finances, for it was the threat of impending governmental bankruptcy that had provoked the summoning of the Estates General. Even before taking the Tennis Court Oath, the Third Estate had declared all existing taxes illegal, since they had not received the consent of the people. The surrender of feudal rights on August 4 brought much relief to the peasants but no revenues to the treasury. Hence the Assembly quickly moved to sweep away the old taxes, both direct and indirect. New sources of revenue were at first hard to come by, whether by issuing new bonds or asking for patriotic contributions, so that despite all efforts, the national debt rose from three to four billion livres during 1789.

One tempting source of wealth lay in the hands of the Church, which was estimated to own perhaps 15 percent of the cultivated land of France. Its total wealth was practically the equivalent of the national debt. An epochal decree of November 1789 provided that all ecclesiastical property was to be transferred to the nation, on condition that the government take over the expenses of worship, salaries of the clergy, and relief of the poor. How was this vast landed wealth to be handled? A decree of December authorized it to be used as a security for the national debt. The government then produced a new financial device, the assignats. Holders of government bonds could exchange these bonds for interest bearing assignats in lieu of cash. Assignats could only be redeemed by purchasing Church lands, and on the completion of such a purchase they would be destroyed. Although the assignats were not legal tender, they unavoidably began to be exchanged as if they were, though with a steadily declining value. By April 1790 they were in fact declared to be negotiable as currency, though by the end of 1791 the assignats as a circulatory medium had lost nearly 25 percent of their face value. The whole experiment has often been held up as a shrewd and insidious financial manipulation that led to an inevitable inflation and that was paid for by the Church, which forfeited all its land. It is to be remembered, of course, that the financial support of the Church was assumed by the state, and that even though the assignats were completely repudiated in 1797 they had saved the day for the government and made possible the orderly transfer of Church property to a new class of possessors.

By 1791 a new basic system of taxation had been created. All internal tariffs and tolls had been abolished, and a general framework of import and export duties was set up at the national frontiers. In place of the old, outrageously unfair tax system, three new taxes were introduced: the universally applicable land tax (*contribution foncière*), the personal property tax (*contribution mobilière*), and a tax on business revenues (*patente*). Though not working very efficiently at first, these were to remain as the essential tax framework of France during the nineteenth century.

A final great matter was that of organized religion. The million or so Protestants in France had had their most glaring disabilities, in existence since Louis XIV's revocation of the Edict of Nantes, removed in 1788. The Declaration of the Rights of Man had proclaimed that no one could be disturbed for his religious opinions. In December 1789 non-Catholics were declared eligible for all public offices. The urgent problem was how to operate the Roman Catholic Church in France once its entire revenues were taken from it and all contemplative monastic orders were abolished. The solution was provided in the document known as the Civil Constitution of the Clergy, voted in the summer of 1790 and reluctantly approved by the king in August.

By this Civil Constitution the number of bishoprics and archbishoprics was almost halved, being reduced to eighty-three, so as to provide one for each department. Many parishes were reorganized and all clerical salaries were assumed by the state. An unprecedented feature was that all clerical positions were to be elective. Bishops were to be chosen in the electoral assemblies of the departments, candidates being obliged to have served as a priest for fifteen years and to be examined in matters of doctrine and morals by their seniors. Parish priests were to be chosen in the electoral assemblies of the districts; they must have been at least five years in holy orders and be approved by their bishop. Nothing apparently would prevent Protestants from joining in the electoral process. After election the incumbent was to take an oath "to be faithful to the nation, to the law, and to the King, and to maintain with all his power the Constitution decreed by the National Assembly."

The Civil Constitution was bitterly denounced by Pope Pius VI, who declared that all clergy taking the civic oath would be suspended by him.

Only seven existing bishops had in fact been willing to take the oath and only about half the parish priests. Thus there came into existence a large class of "nonjuring" clergy. These latter, who could still hold public services if they chose, though without financial support, became increasingly disaffected: some went into the emigration; others remained to form a potential nucleus of revolt in considerable parts of France.

By the early summer of 1791, having proceeded with a marked lack of the disturbances that had occurred in the opening months of the Constituent Assembly, the great work of reorganization seemed to be over. Unhappily, Mirabeau, who had counseled the king to moderation, died in April. Marie Antoinette had always kept closely in touch with her relatives at Vienna, where hostility to the events in France grew daily. The king's two brothers were also closely associated with counterrevolutionary forces abroad. In France much tension was again developing because of inflation, rising prices, and unemployment. In this atmosphere Paris awoke on June 21, 1791, to find itself without a king. After careful preparation, including the building of a specially large coach and the use of disguises, the royal family had managed to escape from the Tuileries, pass undetected through the city gates, and head for the northeast frontier. They were recognized eventually by an innkeeper at Varennes, not far from the Luxembourg border, and were held by local units of the National Guard until an escort could be sent by the Assembly to bring them back to Paris. The return from Varennes was even more unroyal than the transfer from Versailles to Paris in October 1789. Louis was humiliated and mistrusted as never before, so much so that the prospect of his effective service under the constitution about to be launched was remote. Henceforth he and his family were held practically as prisoners in the Tuileries. A crowd, indeed, soon gathered in the Champ-de-Mars to demand his abdication. When dispersed by gunfire, nearly twenty were killed. This "Massacre of the Champ-de-Mars" revived the atmosphere of violence and cast a deep shadow over Louis's formal assent to the constitution in September. On October 1, 1791, when the newly elected Legislative Assembly held its first meeting, the Revolution in one sense was "over," yet at the same time the most ominous portents were arising for the future.

The Failure of the Constitutional Monarchy, 1791–1792

The most obvious word to be associated with the Legislative Assembly which convened at the beginning of October 1791 is failure, for within a year it was gone, France was invaded, and a new era of growing radicalism began. Three main developments marked this critical twelvemonth. Political groupings, if not actual parties, became more clearly defined; social unrest became more prevalent; and growing mistrust abroad of developments in France led in the spring of 1792 to what was to be a vast European war.

The growth of a party system was closely linked to the proliferation of the Paris clubs and owed something perhaps to the facts of architecture. When the deputies were transferred late in 1789 to the royal riding school near the Tuileries, this rectangular building was remodeled so as to place the presiding officer in the middle of one of the longer sides. Government spokesmen and supporters sat by courtesy on his right, the most vehement critics on his left, and a large, indeterminate group of cautious moderates in between. This in itself helped to dramatize the facts of party allegiance. Since a last minute decision of the Constituent Assembly had denied its members the right to stand for reelection, the entire membership now consisted of new men. Many former deputies, however, remained active in the Paris clubs, where as much political activity went on as in the legislature itself. Maximilien Robespierre, for example, a provincial lawyer from Arras who had been a more or less obscure deputy in the Constituent Assembly, quickly rose to be a dominant figure in the Jacobin Club and as such a power in the political world.

Some 264 members of the right have been identified as supporting the Feuillants, a group taking their name from a former convent of that order where they met. They were rivals of the Jacobins and more moderate in outlook. They had as their leaders a triumvirate composed of Barnave, Lameth, and Du Port, as well as such better-known figures as Lafayette and Bailly. From the Feuillants the king selected his first ministry.

Two groups, together numbering about 130 deputies, sat on the left. The majority gathered around Brissot de Warville from Bordeaux. They were consequently known as either the "Bordeaux Group," the "Brissotins," or later the "Girondins." They tended to be members either of the Jacobin Club or the Cordeliers. A still more radical group which accepted the leadership of Robespierre took the name of the Jacobins. In time they were to part company with the Girondins and, though still a minority, to dominate the Revolution. The total numbers of right and left deputies came to nearly 400, though each was a minority. There remained "the Prudent Ones" of the center, numbering nearly 350 and having no precise creed, but prepared to support either right or left as expedience seemed to require.

Economic unrest grew, for the assignats declined in value, while sugar, coffee, and grain prices rose. During the winter of 1791–1792 mobs broke into food warehouses in Paris and elsewhere, while canal barges and wagon trains carrying grain were attacked. The continuation of some of the old feudal money payments perpetuated a resentment which led to sporadic attacks upon landlords. The liberal duke of Rochefoucauld, for example, a friend of George Washington and an honorary citizen of New York, was murdered by a group of peasants on one of his estates.

Above all the domestic issues loomed the increasing menace of the foreign situation. On the whole, enlightened circles in Europe had welcomed the summoning of the Estates General and hailed the fall of the Bastille. But as the attack upon privilege became more vigorous an expected reaction occurred. Marie Antoinette was the sister of Joseph II of Austria who on his death in 1790 was succeeded by his brother Leopold. A revolt in the Austrian Netherlands against Joseph II's innovations had begun in December 1789 and had been warmly welcomed in Paris. Russia and Prussia were troubled at the reform program of their neighboring Polish "patriots." The dynasties of France and Spain were supposedly still closely allied in the Family Compact of 1761, though in the crucial test the compact proved useless. At first selfish concerns kept monarchical Europe from active intervention in French affairs, yet a series of crises soon changed the situation.

These crises were of varied nature. Some German princes, whose feudal rights in Alsace had been guaranteed to them by the Peace of Westphalia, now found these rights abolished and appealed to the Austrian emperor for support. The papal territory of Avignon in the south of France was annexed by the French government in June 1790 after a popular uprising and plebiscite there. When Spain and Britain came to the point of war over their rights to Nootka Sound on the northwest coast of America, France refused to help Spain, despite the Family Compact, and Spain had to back down. The Belgian revolt continued to be enthusiastically hailed in some quarters at Paris to the growing indignation of Vienna.

The steady growth of the emigration, especially in the Rhineland, provided a further element of friction. In November 1790 Edmund Burke published his *Reflections on the Revolution in France*, eloquently denouncing the Revolution which this member of the British Parliament declared had been brought about by what he called "the cannibal philosophers" of France. The book was soon translated and had a powerful influence upon conservative thought in France and Germany. Burke was outraged that any comparison should be made with the Revolution of 1688, which safeguarded England's traditional liberties and thus was in his view essentially "conservative." The new leaders in France, he wrote, "despise experience as the wisdom of unlettered men; and as for the rest, they have wrought under ground a mine that will blow up, at one grand explosion, all examples of antiquity, all precedents, charters, and acts of parliament." Burke was answered in 1791 by Thomas Paine, whose *Rights of Man* vigorously challenged Burke's basic assumptions. "Every generation," Paine wrote, "is, and must be, competent to all the purposes which its occasions require." The rights of man, Paine held, are ascertainable by reason, and civil authority must assert itself to secure these rights.

A final dramatic element was provided by the attempted flight of the royal family in June 1791 and their arrest. Two documents marked the growth of a crisis. In July 1791 the new Emperor Leopold issued a secret circular from Padua to his brother monarchs proposing a joint declaration promising to avenge any "future outrages" in France. In August he and the king of Prussia issued the Declaration of Pillnitz, to the effect that if other monarchs would join them, they were prepared to intervene with force to protect the legitimate rights and interests of the king of France.

Some patriotic Frenchmen, especially among the Brissotins, were by this time clamoring for war. In March 1792 Louis dismissed his Feuillant ministers and turned to the Girondins, whose warlike views now dominated the Legislative Assembly. The chief figure was General Dumouriez, a fanatical opponent of Austria and enough of a royalist to believe that a successful war would quickly restore Louis XVI's fading prestige. Louis XVI, who read the declaration of war to the legislature without any expression of emotion, felt apparently that an Austrian victory would soon mean the restoration of royal authority in France. Thus, it was France that on April 20, and with only seven negative votes, declared war on Austria. The vote included the statement that France, faithful to the principles of its constitution, would not undertake a war of conquests or employ its forces against the liberty of any people.

Though deeper reasons were involved, the war precipitated the fall of the monarchy. The first campaigns went badly for the French, for the weakening of the army due to the resignation of many of the officers' corps had not as yet been offset by the growth of a new national patriotism in the ranks. Louis XVI was unwise enough to veto two decrees of the legislature, following this action by the dismissal of the popular Girondin ministry and its replacement once more by members of the Feuillant group. On June 20, the anniversary of the Tennis Court Oath, a crowd appeared before the Legislative Assembly and submitted a petition protesting the dismissal of the Girondin ministers. Another crowd broke into the Tuileries, found the king, and while not actually harming him forced him to don a revolutionary cap and drink a toast to the nation.

During the summer an Austro-Prussian army commanded by the duke of Brunswick gathered on the northeastern frontier of France. In July the Girondins once again took over the government, obtaining a vote from the Assembly declaring that the country was in danger. An earlier decree had authorized a new army of twenty thousand *fédérés* (local units of the National Guard), and these now began to arrive in Paris, frequently with very radical views. An address submitted to the Assembly by the *fédérés* late in July asked for the suspension of the king. A group from Marseille brought with them a marching song composed by Rouget de Lisle. This was the "Marseillaise," soon to win immortality as one of the greatest of all patriotic anthems.

Early in August a manifesto issued by the duke of Brunswick, demanding that all Frenchmen submit and threatening to destroy Paris totally if any harm was done to the royal family, was published in the *Moniteur*. This spelled the doom of the monarchy. On the night of August 9–10 organized risings throughout Paris replaced the older city government with a new revolutionary Commune. New officials took over, and on their orders crowds assaulted the Tuileries, losing about ninety dead and massacring some six hundred of the king's loyal Swiss Guards. Louis and his family took refuge with the Assembly, where as semiprisoners they listened to the night-long debate. At the end it was voted to suspend the monarchy, establish a Provisional Executive Council of six ministers, and elect a new National Convention on the basis of universal manhood suffrage to devise republican institutions for France. For the security of the royal family it was decided to detain them in the Temple—a forbidding medieval structure once the home of the Knights Templars.

Three bodies now divided power among themselves: the Legislative Assembly, the Revolutionary Commune of Paris, and the new Provisional Executive Council. This last was dominated by Georges Jacques Danton, the new minister of justice. A lawyer from the provinces, Danton had been president of the Cordeliers Club and one of the most eloquent speakers at the Jacobins. As minister of justice his first duty was to rally the country against the invaders. This he did with superb eloquence.[4] Pressure from the Commune forced dramatic social and economic changes. All remaining feudal land dues were to be abolished without compensation unless the proprietor could produce the original title, all common lands were declared to belong to village communities, and *émigré* land was in principle subject to confiscation. Registration of births, marriages, and deaths was transferred from the clergy to municipal authorities while legislation was introduced also on the subject of divorce.

Once again violence and bloodshed appeared. Suspicion and unrest in

---

[4] Danton, whose statue stands on the Boulevard Saint-Germain, is one of the few revolutionary leaders thus to be prominently commemorated in Paris. Robespierre has no such memorial.

Paris led the Assembly to create a vigilance committee which undertook house-to-house searches and arrests. Powers were delegated to the various *sections* of Paris, an immediate consequence of which was the crowding of all Paris prisons with suspects. The duke of Brunswick's invasion had begun, and by August 26 the news had reached Paris that the great frontier fortress of Longwy had traitorously capitulated. On September 1 further news came that Verdun also was about to fall. This was the precipitant of one of the bloodiest episodes in the entire history of the French Revolution. Crowds "visited" prison after prison, all packed with suspects. In some cases the inmates were simply hacked to death in cold blood; in other cases perfunctory hearings were held in the prison courtyards. The results in either case were the same: a hideous bloodletting with piles of mutilated corpses left in every prison yard in Paris. The total number of these ghastly executions has been estimated at around twelve hundred, or about half of the total prison population. Equally savage massacres occurred in the provinces, so that this, as much as anything else, has contributed to the picture of the Revolution as an orgy of mass violence. As minister of justice, Danton certainly condoned, if he did not initiate, what occurred. Editors of Paris newspapers such as Jean Paul Marat, who recklessly published incitements to violence, share the responsibility.

On the very day, September 20, 1792, when the Legislative Assembly was to turn over its powers to a Convention elected under the shadow of these bloody events, the invading armies of the duke of Brunswick met the French near the little town of Valmy, less than a hundred miles from Paris. A cannonade, by which the defenders responded to the Prussian advance during the morning mists, was the essence of the battle. For whatever reason—dysentery, muddy roads, bad weather, or poor morale— Brunswick ordered a retreat, which did not stop until the invading armies had reached the frontier. Thus the "cannonade" of Valmy, unimpressive in contrast to the great military conflicts of the past, became one of the decisive battles of history. Paris was saved, and the Revolution, hitherto on the defensive, quickly took on an aggressive, crusading character.

More immediately significant was the fact that the Legislative Assembly, intended to be the permanent, formally established government of a new France, now came to a premature end, giving place to a constitutionally unauthorized body, the Convention, under which France was to move into new and more revolutionary situations. All the burdens of the new age were to rest on its shoulders. Yet, though the Legislative Assembly ended in failure, the great constructive work of the years 1789–1791 remained. The Assembly had found time to confer honorary citizenship upon Tom Paine, Washington, Hamilton, Madison, Jeremy Bentham, Wilberforce, Pestalozzi, and the Polish patriot Kosciuszko. Talleyrand had submitted a comprehensive plan for public primary and secondary education to the Constituent Assembly as early as September 1791; and on the very day (April 20, 1792) when the Legislative Assembly declared war, it received from Condorcet a report on education which has been described as a landmark in French educational history. In a mingled atmosphere of constructive achievement, foreign menace, and growing domestic violence the Legislative Assembly dissolved itself less than a year from its beginning.

4

THE FIRST
FRENCH REPUBLIC

Making the Republic, 1792–1793

Cumulative violence at home combined with the alarming war crisis on the northeast frontier in the late summer of 1792 spelled the doom of the French monarchy. What had been "suspension" in the August crisis soon turned to the formal abolition of the thousand-year-old kingship when the Convention met late in September. In theory if not in fact the voice of the people for the first time in French history was now supreme. Though the Republic thus created was in time to be overthrown, it had an obvious parentage and affiliation with those regimes that followed, down to the Fifth Republic of 1958, so that again and again throughout the nineteenth and twentieth centuries the battles of the first great Revolution were to be refought.

Born amid violence, the First Republic of 1792 continued its stormy way amid ever greater violence. In popular mythology the year beginning in the summer of 1793 was marked by the ascendancy of the Jacobins, and the bloody phenomenon of the Reign of Terror which then exploded

◀ THE ACTOR CHENARD IN SANS-CULOTTE COSTUME, BY BOILLY *Made for the festival celebrating the incorporation of French Savoy in October 1792, the painting shows the typical* sans-culotte *costume—wooden sabots, neckerchief, and ragged clothing. The inscription on the tricolor reads "Liberty or Death." Boilly was the most famous of the revolutionary popular artists.*

sometimes has been taken to constitute the veritable "French Revolution." It is clear, however, that the truly meaningful changes had been made in 1789, for in that year the legislation was undertaken which gave the French people the basic civil rights and the essential administrative structure which they still have. To these early reforms were later to be added the further changes of the year 1800 when Bonaparte as First Consul quickly demonstrated his genius in consolidating the reforms of a decade earlier and in adding to them his own contributions to order and stability.

What gave a distinctive element to the years 1792–1795 was the increased activity of "the people." The great preceding reforms had been won largely by enlightened aristocrats and liberal members of the bourgeoisie. Recent scholarship has been able to show that even the new popular movements involved not so much a "gutter proletariat" as they did the "little people," the *menu peuple*. The term *sans-culottes* then widely applied to them included the craftsmen, shopkeepers, small workshop masters, and journeymen most strongly concentrated and organized in Paris.[1] The period was marked by the continuing pressure of the communal government of Paris, the vigorous local political activity of its *sections*, and indeed almost everywhere throughout France the assertiveness of the new democratic local authorities. Leaders in the Convention, if not themselves literally *menu peuple*, became increasingly their champions. What is also significant about the years 1792–1795 was a certain element of myth with phrases such as "The country in danger," "The people in arms," "Death to the tyrant," on everyone's lips. This myth was accompanied by two striking phenomena: one was the technique of revolutionary dictatorship, most notably employed by Robespierre; the other was the repeated concomitant manifestation of popular democracy, seen most widely in the actions of the Paris crowds (one should be careful not to limit oneself to the term *mob*), and somewhat less dramatically in the thousand exercises of similar power in towns and villages throughout France. Here was something unknown in the past that would leave a permanent legacy for the future.

The National Convention which assembled on September 20, 1792, was a wholly republican body. The decree of the preceding legislature which authorized it wiped out the distinction between active and passive citizens, so that in theory all Frenchmen of twenty-one and over were entitled to vote. Election was still by two stages (voters choosing electors and electors

---

[1] *Sans-culottes* (literally "without breeches") is the term for those who spurned the costume of the old aristocracy to wear the pantaloons typical of the artisan class. Two recent basic works have given new emphasis to the role of the *sans-culottes:* G. Rudé, *The Crowd in the French Revolution* (1959), and A. Soboul, *The Parisian Sans-Culottes and the French Revolution, 1793–1794* (1964).

choosing deputies); in the confusions of the times, however, not more than a tenth of those eligible went to the polls. In Paris, where balloting began on the first day of the September prison massacres, the results showed a sharp swing to the left, and the same phenomenon was widespread. New tides were sweeping a republican and theoretically democratic France into unknown waters. Since the basic structural changes as well as those concerning taxation, the army, and the courts had already been made, for three years France had to wrestle with problems that were increasingly social and economic in nature and always complicated by the urgent pressures of an ever-larger European war.

More than had been true before, the elements of a party system began to emerge. The Convention moved at this time from the riding school to the old royal theater within the Tuileries, remodeled to accommodate the 750 deputies. A compact body of about 165 Girondins, sitting on the right and having the temporary support of the majority of the center group, was in control. Brissot, a journalist and advocate of good causes even before the Revolution (he was one of the founders of the Society of the Friends of the Blacks), was still the chief leader of the group. Condorcet, a friend of Lafayette and Sieyès and one of the oldest of the Girondins, was truly a philosophe of the *ancien régime;* he was one of the few, indeed, of that breed actually to see the Revolution. He served as vice-president of the Convention. Roland, who had earlier been minister of war, was now eclipsed by his youthful wife, Manon, whose drawing room became a lively center for the discussion of party matters both theoretical and practical.

Seated on the high benches to the left of the president was a compact body of some ninety Jacobins nicknamed, because of their position, "the Mountain." The opposition of Girondins and Jacobins is historic, though it was perhaps as much a conflict of personalities as it was a disagreement on essential republican goals. Differences to be sure did exist. The Girondins tended to be men of property, cultivated theorists somewhat aloof from the common man whose cause they professed to champion. They were highly suspicious of the leadership of Paris and disliked the repeated violence which surged up in its streets. For this reason they were bitterly opposed by the Jacobins who drew much of their support from the Paris *sections* and who in turn accused the Girondins of weakening France by trying to create a loosely federal state. In the early summer of 1793 the Jacobins were to destroy their opponents and attempt to create that remarkable structure, the Jacobin Commonwealth.

Although often charged with a sort of academic idealism, the Girondins have substantial achievements to their credit. On September 21, 1792, with a notable lack of fervor, the Convention declared monarchy abolished. All public documents were to be dated from "the first year of the French Republic." Only in this indirect way was the official republican title established. In the second place, they undertook to settle the fate of the king. Pushed hard in this respect by the Jacobins, in December they brought "Louis Capet," as he was called, to trial. A safe containing copies of large numbers of letters to *émigrés* and foreign courts had been found in the Tuileries, and these were the basis for the charge of treason brought against him. The trial, in which Louis was loyally and ably defended by Malesherbes, a distinguished lawyer of the *ancien régime*, and in which the king conducted himself with much dignity, lasted over a month. In the end a unanimous Convention found him guilty, and by a small majority—387 to 334—sentenced him to death. Since 26 of those in favor of the death penalty were opposed to immediate execution, it is possible to say that the vote for immediate execution had a majority of only one. Louis met his fate on the guillotine bravely on January 21, 1793, in a Paris that was startled and perhaps even astounded at what had occurred.

In the third place, the Girondins vigorously pursued a war that was steadily broadening in scope and changing in nature. Valmy had been the great turning point. By the end of 1792 three republican armies had crossed the frontier: Dumouriez in the Austrian Netherlands, Custine in the Rhineland, and Montesquiou and Anselme in Savoy and Nice. The propaganda aspect of the war also changed, for France was no longer engaged simply in repelling the invader. A decree of November promised, "fraternity and aid to all people wishing to recover their liberty," and another decree of December announced that the French armies would bring their new institutions to the lands which they occupied. In January 1793 Danton made a dramatic statement to the Convention to the effect that the frontiers of France were those designed by nature. After local plebiscites, Nice and Savoy were declared annexed to France as were a number of towns in the Rhineland and the Austrian Netherlands which had also voted for annexation. Such actions broadened the scope of the war. England, concerned at the execution of the king and the occupation of the Low Countries by French troops, broke off diplomatic relations. France declared war on England and Holland in February 1793. Soon afterwards Spain, Portugal, Sardinia, Tuscany, and Naples, all concerned at the new threats to the old order, also declared war. A First Coalition had come into existence, strengthened by the subsidies which William Pitt, the English prime minister, furnished to his allies. It was the first of five coalitions that were to carry on the great struggle with only slight interruptions until in 1815 Napoleon was finally dethroned.

The much enlarged war did not go well for France. Custine was forced back along the Rhine, while Dumouriez blamed the government for the failure of his plans in the Netherlands. He first sought to march on Paris and restore the monarchy, but when his men would not follow him he deserted to the Austrians. At the same time a revolt broke out in the western parts of France known as the Vendée, where the conservative, royalist influence of the nobility and nonjuring clergy was strongest. Unrest was also present in other ways, for food prices took a sharp upward turn in the spring of 1793. Widespread riots occurred in Paris in February and such disturbances continued, encouraged by the group of extremists known as the *Enragés* (the "madmen"). These riots were directly associated with the economic problems of the working classes. The principal demands were for coffee, sugar, soap, and candles. Again and again crowds burst into shops, refusing to pay more than from one-tenth to one-third of the inflated prices of such commodities. Bread was no longer a critical commodity, for the city authorities held its price down temporarily by subsidies to bakers. Though the Girondins were theoretically in favor of *laissez-faire*, they were compelled under such pressures to adopt a whole series of emergency measures. In the economic sphere they first imposed a special levy on the rich. After a crowd of ten thousand appeared before the Convention early in May demanding control of food prices, that body voted the first Law of the Maximum, authorizing local authorities to set maximum prices for grain. Efforts were made to maintain order. The old decrees against *émigrés* were consolidated and made harsher. A new criminal court, the Revolutionary Tribunal, was set up. In April a new executive committee of nine members, the Committee of Public Safety, was also authorized. Delegates known as representatives on mission, were sent to the departments and to the armies to stimulate loyalty and root out suspects. Local Watch Committees were authorized for the same purpose. Such measures, which antedated the pattern of revolutionary government soon to be developed by the Jacobins, represented not so much a considered Girondin policy as a response to the critical pressures of the moment.

Discontent with the government came to a head in May. Its Jacobin opponents, who had been able to repudiate the moderate draft of a proposed new republican constitution prepared by the Girondins, mobilized the local Paris *sections*. These were able to give the communal government of the capital an even more revolutionary character. A Central Revolutionary Committee, made up of delegates from the forty-eight *sections*, established itself in permanence near the end of May. In addition to the existing National Guard it raised and armed a new revolutionary militia of twenty thousand. The tocsin was rung on May 31 to bring force to bear against the Girondin government, but at first with little response. Then on June 2 (Sunday) a huge crowd of eighty thousand made up of units of the

National Guard, the new revolutionary militia, and ordinary citizens massed in the courtyard of the Tuileries. It was equipped with 150 cannons. Although one of the largest mass demonstrations of the entire Revolution, it was also one of the least bloody, for the government had neither the desire nor the ability to resist. The majority of the Convention, now swinging to the Jacobin side, voted to place twenty-nine leading Girondin deputies and two ministers under house arrest. Many others, including Condorcet and Roland, went into hiding, so that the way was now clear for the Jacobins to take control.

The Rule of the Jacobins, 1793–1794

The great threat of popular violence which led to the fall of the Girondins in June 1793 meant the arrival of another minority, the Jacobins, at the center of power. They were to exercise this power for just one year. The period is marked by the climax of the radical revolution at home and by an even greater enlargement of the war. Ruthless measures were taken to put down revolts in the provinces. In Paris a tightly organized Jacobin dictatorship was at the helm, seeking to bring about a new world. Its programs were undertaken in an atmosphere of heightened violence (this was the period of the First and Second Terror) which antagonized large parts of Europe more than ever before, to say nothing of the *émigrés* who had left France.

The Jacobins provide an early illustration of the revolutionary exercise of power. Their club in Paris had grown steadily more radical. During 1790 and 1791 local societies had grown up closely linked with the parent organization, so that ultimately an estimated sixty-eight hundred Jacobin clubs existed with perhaps half a million members. Studies of membership show a wide spectrum of occupations. Petty tradesmen and skilled artisans formed the substantial central grouping, with smaller elements drawn from the lawyers, professional and businessmen, former clergy, and army officers at one end of the spectrum and day laborers and peasants at the other.

The Paris club was a powerful pressure group, for it could work directly upon the Convention. Local clubs were kept closely in touch through correspondence and were regularly exhorted to action. In this way they became a semiofficial part of the government, acting as agents of surveillance and denouncing traitors. A good deal of ritual developed. The Jacobins were tireless in commemorating the new national festivals, erecting altars to *la patrie*, singing patriotic songs, and planting trees of liberty. In many respects they tended to substitute the religion of patriotism for that of the traditional Church. They were of necessity republican but hardly, as is sometimes claimed, socialists. The Jacobin membership included many to whom the Revolution had brought real benefits, not the least of those benefits being the chance to acquire some patch of landed property. In general, therefore, they would support the institutions of private property and *laissez-faire*, though at times they associated themselves with a greater degree of radical change than their theoretical beliefs could justify.

The great Jacobin figures were Danton, Marat, Saint-Just, and Robespierre. Danton was easily the most prominent at first, for with his commanding physical presence and powerful gifts of oratory he had rallied France in 1792 against the mortal danger of invasion and had seemed to personify the Republic. Yet this solicitor from Arcis-sur-Aube, who had become an outstanding member of the radical Cordeliers Club, had also accumulated a substantial fortune through speculation and various obscure financial dealings. He fell out of favor with his colleagues and in July 1793 asked to leave the Committee of Public Safety. Eight months later Robespierre was to bring him to the guillotine.

Jean Paul Marat was a strange and strikingly different type. He was a medical doctor with an honorary degree from St. Andrew's University in Scotland, and he had published various monographs on scientific and political subjects, the latter showing an indebtedness to Montesquieu, Beccaria, and Rousseau. He lived in one of the poorest sections of Paris, dressed like a cutthroat, and in 1789 founded *L'Ami du Peuple*, a newspaper which was bloodthirsty, vituperative, and, possibly because of this, intensely popular. He represented his *section* in the Convention and in April 1793 had been president of the Paris Jacobin Club. Four months later a country girl, Charlotte Corday, ignoring his humanitarian professions and regarding him as the enemy of his country, went to his house and stabbed him while in his bath. In death Marat became one of the greatest of the revolutionary martyrs. David painted a famous portrait, and prints of him were sold everywhere in Paris.

Still another type was Saint-Just, a young country attorney elected a deputy to the Convention at the age of twenty-four. Devoted to Robespierre, he became within a year a member of the Committee of Public Safety. Saint-Just combined passionate oratory with a fanatical zeal. "One does not," he declared, "make revolutions by halves." As a special emissary to the armies he never hesitated to destroy those whom he considered to be enemies of the Republic. "Punish not only traitors, but even the indifferent," he declared. At the age of twenty-six he died loyally with Robespierre on the guillotine.

Maximilien de Robespierre held a unique position, for more than any other he seemed the embodiment of Jacobinism. He was a country lawyer from Arras whose early activities in the local debating and reading societies had made him a devotee of Voltaire, Raynal, and above all Rousseau. Because of his membership in the Constituent Assembly he was denied a place in the Legislative Assembly, playing instead a most active role in the Paris Jacobin Club. Elected to the Convention, he rapidly became the principal spokesman for the Jacobins and for nearly a year the master of France. Paradoxes seem to abound in Robespierre. He never abandoned the conservative dress, the powdered hair, and the prim manner of his early years. At the time of wild financial speculation and almost universal corruption he was accurately called "the Incorruptible," living in a single modest room near the Tuileries in the quiet circle of a carpenter's family. He died a poor man. From Rousseau he accepted the ideas of natural rights, popular sovereignty, the reign of virtue, and a simple civic religion. In contrast he combined with these ideas the most cold-blooded ruthlessness in destroying those he believed were opposed to him. Desmoulins, with whom he had been at school and at whose wedding he had been a witness, he sent to the guillotine. "Virtue," he once said, "is always in a minority," and he acted unhesitatingly upon this principle.

The problem of the Jacobins was to put their ideas into effect at a time of not one but several major crises. An immediate question was that of the Girondin draft of a new constitution for France, for which the Jacobins quickly substituted their own more radical version. Had this Jacobin Constitution of 1793 gone into effect, France would have been governed by a single-chamber legislature elected by universal manhood suffrage and completely renewed every year. Among the rights asserted in the constitution were public assistance to the unemployed, aged, and infirm, and public education for all. A system of popular referendum and recall was also provided. The drastic document was voted by the Convention in June, overwhelmingly ratified by plebiscite in August,[2] and conveniently and permanently shelved by the Convention in October. The stresses of the time required this, for as a resolution then declared, "the provisional government of France is revolutionary until the peace."

The first major problem for the Jacobins was the Federalist Revolt, which made alarming progress in the summer of 1793. The Girondins, always suspicious of Paris, had many sympathizers in the country, where sixty of the eighty-three departments were in more or less open revolt. By the end of July the major opposition had been put down, though Lyon remained hostile until October and Toulon was not won back until

[2] By a vote of 1,801,908 to 11,610.

December. In this atmosphere it seemed imperative to the Jacobins that they continue and, indeed, enlarge their system of emergency dictatorial government.

The Jacobin system of revolutionary government is a classic example of the means employed by a minority to exercise power in a revolutionary situation. The essential technique was to concentrate authority in a series of self-perpetuating committees only nominally subject to an elected legislature or to the people. Chronologically, the beginning came with the suspension of the monarchy in August 1792, when the Provisional Executive Council, first dominated by Danton, was set up. This soon declined in authority when the Convention met. During the ascendancy of the Girondins a number of emergency steps were taken. A Committee of General Security, first set up by the Convention in October 1792 to supervise police activities, was enlarged in the spring of 1793. More important was the Committee of Public Safety, set up by decree in April 1793. This committee of ultimately twelve members of the Convention sitting for renewable terms of one month was entrusted with complete administrative powers and soon became Jacobin dominated. Supposedly making weekly reports to the Convention, it made little of this obligation and soon became the supreme agent of Jacobin power, controlled by the personality of Robespierre.[3] Still another agency was the Revolutionary Tribunal, created in March 1793 to combat all counterrevolutionary activities. In final form it had sixteen judges and sixty jurors, divided into four sections, as well as a public prosecutor, the notorious Fouquier-Tinville. Various laws were passed to strengthen the powers of this court which between March 1793 and July 1794 sentenced some twenty-six hundred men and women to death. Similar tribunals were authorized in the chief departmental cities. Another device, first employed in March 1793 was that of the representatives on mission, and still another was that of the local Watch Committees. These originally Girondin creations were given greatly expanded powers.

Along with this formal machinery of government went the calculated exercise of terror to destroy the opponents of the regime. A vote of September 5, 1793, placed "Terror" on the order of the day. This meant that the guillotine became established in permanence at Paris in what are now the Place de la Concorde and the Place de la Nation. The major cities of France were similarly equipped. The First Terror, which ran through the closing half of 1793 and into 1794 saw some twenty thousand people lose their lives—not all, to be sure through the formal process of trial and the guillotine. An even more savage Second Terror was to be crowded

[3] R. R. Palmer's *Twelve Who Ruled* (Princeton, 1959) is a masterly account of its work.

into the two months of June and July 1794 and to result ultimately in Robespierre's own downfall. Combining the period of the two Terrors and counting those who died in prison and met death in other ways without trial, an estimate of between thirty-five thousand and forty thousand has been reached. The Terror was not directed against the aristocratic class as such; it was "socially indiscriminate but politically perspicacious," that is to say, it would destroy people of any class who were thought to be opposed to the Republic.[4] In September 1793 a Law of Suspects authorized the immediate arrest of those who "by their conduct, association, talk, or writings have shown themselves partisans of tyranny." In October the government of France was declared to be "revolutionary until peace."

Finally, the Convention voted in December 1793 the document which came to be known as the Constitution of the Terror. It specified in elaborate detail how every operation of government, central or local, military, civil, or diplomatic, was to be drawn within the orbit of the National Convention, and more precisely within the surveillance of the two great Committees. The phrases recur monotonously:

> All constituted bodies are under the immediate inspection of the Committee of Public Safety. . . . Active supervision relative to military laws and measures, to administrative, civil, and criminal laws is delegated to the Executive Council which shall render account thereof in writing, every ten days, to the Committee of Public Safety. . . . Each and every minister is required personally to give a special and summary account . . . every ten days to the Committee of Public Safety. . . . The supervision of the execution of revolutionary laws . . . is attributed exclusively to the districts upon condition of rendering an accurate account thereof to the Committee of Public Safety. . . . The application of military measures appertains to the generals . . . upon express condition of rendering account every ten days, to the Executive Council. . . . The application of revolutionary laws and measures of general security . . . is entrusted to the municipalities and to the Watch or Revolutionary Committees on condition also of reporting every ten days on the execution of such laws in the district of their arrondissement. . . . The Representatives of the People [on mission] shall correspond every ten days with the Committee of Public Safety.

[4] See Donald Greer, *The Incidence of the Terror* (1935).

In a still further sweeping allotment of authority it was stipulated that "the Committee of Public Safety is specially charged with major diplomatic operations." Such was the machinery, essentially dictatorial and ruthless, by which France was governed.

The year of Jacobin ascendancy saw a striking body of legislation directed to economic and social ends. In the preceding Girondin period the assignats had been made legal tender, an attempt had been made to fix a maximum price for grain, and peasants had been given some help in purchasing confiscated *émigré* land. The further steps taken by the Jacobins were undoubtedly influenced by the September crisis, that is to say, the continuing civil strife in the Vendée and the misfortunes of the war, where Mainz was lost in August and Toulon in September. Popular agitation in Paris, by no means always satisfied with the Jacobin leadership, stressed the ever-present food shortages and the rising prices. In July 1793 the last feudal dues owed by peasant landholders were declared abolished without compensation. In September a compulsory loan was imposed upon wealthy citizens proportionate to their income. The Great Law of the Maximum, also enacted in September and going much beyond the earlier measure, established uniform prices in France for thirty-nine commodities, including all major foodstuffs, paper, hides, metals, cloths, soap, candles, and tobacco. Maximum prices were to be fixed in each district, usually at those of 1790 plus one-third. Maximum wages were to be fixed by the general councils of the communes at the average 1790 level plus one-half. In October a special Commission of Supplies was authorized with power over the producing, transporting, importing, and exporting of agricultural and industrial products. It is also significant that in October the Paris Commune introduced ration cards for bread.

Another form of mobilization was the *levée en masse*, proclaimed in August 1793. It had been preceded by a military *levée* of 300,000 in February 1793. Since this new measure now made all unmarried men between the ages of eighteen and twenty-five liable for immediate military service, it can be regarded in a sense as the beginning of all modern systems of military conscription. By midsummer French military effectives were at the previously unheard of figure of 650,000 men. The implications were very much wider, since the Committee of Public Safety was charged with the duty of setting up workshops and factories to make arms and munitions, of commandeering supplies, and of requisitioning workmen and technicians. In glowing language it was announced that all Frenchmen and women were to be mustered in the service of the state:

> The young men shall go to battle; the married men shall
> forge arms and transport provisions; women will make tents

and clothes, and serve in hospitals; children will turn rags
into lint; old men will get themselves carried to public
places, there to stir up the courage of warriors, hatred of
kings, and unity in the Republic.

Other economic measures included the Navigation Act of September
1793 which severely limited the right of foreign merchant ships to carry
goods in and out of France, and the Embargo Act of October prohibiting
all English merchandise from the soil of France. While hardly a war
measure, one must note also the decree of August 1793 establishing a uniform, decimal system of weights and measures, the meter being set at one
ten-millionth of the distance from the equator to the North Pole.[5]
In this enlarging atmosphere of governmental control, other important
steps were taken. A decree of February 1794 abolished all slavery in the
French colonies, the former slaves becoming citizens of the French Republic. In March 1794 the Ventôse Decrees (from the name of the month
in the new revolutionary calendar) stipulated that local communes should
draw up lists of needy patriots who should be given the property confiscated from the enemies of the Republic.
None of this legislation long survived the fall of the Robespierrists in
the summer of 1794. In essence these were emergency measures, respond-
ing to popular needs and destined to be discarded when the crisis was
over. "The men of the Convention," three of the most distinguished
scholars of his period have asserted, "became in the end that which fundamentally they had never ceased to be: individualists akin to those of
the Constituent Assembly, and akin to those whom the eighteenth century had formed. Free from the political and social pressures of 1793–
1794, they returned to the economic standpoint of 1790." [6]
As Robespierre, the dominant figure of the Committee of Public
Safety, presided over these social and economic innovations, he was concerned also with what has been perhaps ironically described as "the Republic of Virtue." A new France—indeed, a new world—so he thought,
was being born. The new revolutionary calendar, the work of a special
technical committee set up for that purpose, was authorized in October
1793 though its dating went back to the previous year. September 22,
1792, the day following the abolition of monarchy, therefore became the
first day of "the Year I of the French Republic." In complete disregard
of the rest of the world, and of the Sundays, the feast days, and the saints'

---

[5] The full elaboration of the metric system had to await the law of December 1799.
[6] R. Mousnier, E. Labrousse, and M. Bouloiseau, *Le XVIIIe Siècle* (Paris, 1955),
p. 427.

days of the Roman Catholic Church, the year was divided into twelve months of thirty days each, with five (or six) holidays at the close. Each month was divided into three "decades" of ten days apiece (*Primidi, Duodi, Tridi,* and so on to *Décadi*). A markedly poetic flavor was given by its author, Fabre d'Eglantine, to the calendar of months. The three autumnal months were *Vendémiaire, Brumaire,* and *Frimaire;* the winter months, *Nivôse, Pluviôse,* and *Ventôse;* the spring months, *Germinal, Floréal,* and *Prairial;* the summer months, *Messidor, Thermidor,* and *Fructidor.* The revolutionary dating, with all its confusions, remained in use for more than a decade until Napoleon finally restored the Gregorian calendar in January 1806.

The powerful initiative taken by the leaders of the Convention was assisted by a striking growth of popular activity. Recent studies have given much attention to the *sans-culottes,* those lesser people through whose actions it is possible to see the Revolution "from below." Active in the Paris *sections,* where endless duties were expected from them on local revolutionary committees, and also active in the popular societies which sprang up everywhere, the *sans-culottes* were the exponents of direct democracy, which they took to be simply the popular application of the essential principles of the Revolution. Holding that the people were sovereign and entitled to liberty and equality, they championed the autonomy of their *section* assemblies against the rule of the Convention or at times even the machinery of the Jacobin dictatorship. The *sans-culottes* had helped to bring the Jacobins to power; they were incessant in their fear of hunger and in their demand for measures to avert it. Yet ultimately their popular democracy became intolerable to the so-called bourgeois democracy, which was in reality the Jacobin dictatorship. Robespierre sent the *Hébertistes,* those demanding the most radical social reforms, to the guillotine.

The *sans-culottes* covered a wide range of occupations—petty merchants, craftsmen, salaried employees, day laborers, and the like—and they affected a costume suggestive of the revolutionary age. This typically included trousers striped in red and blue, a shirt open at the neck, a short, loose jacket (the *carmagnole*), a red "Phrygian" cap of liberty, and frequently wooden shoes as a gesture towards saving leather for the army. The *sans-culottes* insisted upon the right of every citizen to bear arms, and since the musket and saber were not always obtainable they generally carried what came to be the most typical weapon of the Revolution, the pike. Women's dress was unassuming, and the hair of both sexes was dressed simply and unpowdered.

Both legal enactments and popular enthusiasm led to further striking changes. Not only inherited titles, but even the terms "monsieur" and "madame" were banned, these being replaced by the simple appellation of "citizen." The pronoun "tu," once limited to the family and to domestics, drove out the more formal "vous." In a thousand small ways—through prints, ornaments, placards, jewelry, chinaware, pipes, busts, souvenir stones from the Bastille, playing cards—a new age was given its symbolism. Even proper names were changed, with those taken from Roman republican heroes such as Brutus or Gracchus highly popular. Some of the *sections* of Paris chose to rename themselves with titles such as "Marat," "Liberty Bonnet," "Unity," "Social Contract," or "Sans-Culottes." Many towns and villages similarly asserted their patriotism. At least forty towns added the word "Egalité" to the original name; Compiègne became "Marat-sur-Oise"; Auteuil became "Auteuil-sans-Culottes"; and one village chose to become "Brutus the Magnanimous." Furniture design broke away from the traditional elegance of Louis XV and Louis XVI styles, now held to be effete, and turned for its models to antiquity, particularly to Rome and Pompeii. Painting, too, became proudly republican in the classical manner under the leadership of Jacques David, who in addition to being the official painter of this age served under the Convention as a member of the Committee of General Security. Still another example of the new current was the theater, which was never more popular than in these turbulent years, taking on, as could be expected, a vehemently propagandist flavor. The Convention, for example, decreed in August 1793 that three times a week at certain designated places there should be played "The tragedies of *Brutus, William Tell* and *Caius Gracchus*—retracing the glorious events of the Revolution and the virtues of the defenders of liberty." A severe censorship kept everything in line. Popular music, most notably the patriotic "Marseillaise," the military "Ça ira," and "Dansons la Carmagnole," also dramatized the Republican cause.

These semispontaneous changes were accompanied by carefully organized public festivals and manifestations. Many of these were in the field of religion. As early as November 1792 the Cathedral of Notre Dame had become a "Temple of Reason" with an actress from the *Comédie Française* presiding as its goddess, in a decorous ceremony none the less shocking to some traditional opinion. Local policy was frequently very hostile to the worship authorized by the Civil Constitution of the Clergy. The Paris Commune, for example, ordered the closing of all churches in November 1793. Robespierre himself ardently encouraged revolutionary religious symbolism. He was responsible for the decree of May 1794 establishing the worship of the Supreme Being and calling upon all Frenchmen to recognize only two dogmas, the existence of the Supreme Being and the immortality of the soul. A list of official public festivals throughout the year was announced, as well as minor festivals on the tenth day of each "decade."

The great Festival of the Supreme Being was one of the most spectacular examples of such revolutionary symbolism. It was elaborately organized, with special music and white-clad, flower-bedecked choirs vigorously trained in the Paris *sections* and having a *décor* worked out by David himself. For the vast ceremony an artificial mountain was built in the Champ-de-Mars and strewn with objects of revolutionary symbolism. In the Tuileries gardens between huge stands for the deputies was erected a cloth and plaster statue of Atheism to which Robespierre, after all the parading and after the singing of patriotic hymns, set fire. This having been ignited, another statue, of Wisdom, arose through the smoke, unsteady and scorched yet triumphant over its rival descending to oblivion amid the flames. This most dramatic moment in Robespierre's public career, so heavily laden with all the symbolism of the Revolution, came less than two months before his fall.

Important progress was made by the Jacobins in the field of foreign affairs. When they took office in June 1793 the war quite clearly was not going well. The change came during the autumn. The victory at Hondschoote in September stopped a British advance in the Low Countries; and in December, thanks in part to the skill of a young artillery officer, Captain Bonaparte, Toulon was recaptured. The great assembling of new troops as the result of the *levée en masse* gave Carnot, its director, the sobriquet, "Organizer of Victory." This was more than simply a name, for the French victory at Fleurus in June 1794 opened the way for a second overrunning of the Austrian Netherlands.

Despite all such achievements, the Robespierrists by the summer of 1794 were close to destruction. They had pinned much of their hopes upon the Terror, first in the closing half of 1793 and again, with much greater fury, in June and July of 1794. During these two months, and with the new ferocious June Law of Prairial which denied the accused practically any means of defense, almost as many guillotinings occurred in Paris as in the whole year preceding.

Robespierre and his small group of devoted followers lost control of France—and their lives—because of the situation which they themselves had created. Robespierre can be seen today not as a bloodthirsty monster but as a strange type of idealist who had aborbed Rousseau's ideas of political society guaranteeing the natural rights of all men; he had combined this belief with Rousseau's naturalistic personal faith in a Supreme Being "who protects the oppressed and punishes the oppressors" (Robespierre's words). To realize these views he was prepared temporarily to suspend the very institutions in which he fundamentally believed and to act as long as necessary as a dictator. Thus he had to destroy the factions organized against him, whether *Enragés*, *Hébertistes*, or *Dantonistes*. The Hébertists had been guillotined in March 1793 on the grounds of plotting a popular insurrection. The Dantonists followed in April, charged with financial intrigues and conspiracy with aliens abroad. Inevitably, however, this policy led to bitter opposition within Robespierre's own party. The Law of Prairial, designed to impose the death penalty upon all "enemies of the people," no longer allowed deputies to be exempted because of any parliamentary privilege. It is understandable, therefore, that some of Robespierre's fellow Jacobins felt that he was in essence declaring war upon them and decided to strike back. On July 27 (the ninth Thermidor) the conspirators found courage to denounce Robespierre in the Convention and to obtain his arrest along with his closest associates. That night only thirteen of the forty-eight Paris *sections* rallied to his support after Robespierre and the other prisoners had escaped and made their new headquarters at the Hôtel de Ville. Here troops sent by the Convention late at night seized the leaders. Robespierre, his jaw broken by a pistol shot, was carried on a shutter through the streets to the Tuileries, lying there through the night in agony on a table in the ante-room of the Committee of Public Safety while his fate was decided within. Next day, he, Saint-Just, and twenty others were sent to the guillotine where they had sent thousands before them. An epoch was over.

The Thermidorean Reaction, 1794–1795

The month of Thermidor has given its name to the men and the period that succeeded. The Thermidoreans were those surviving Jacobins now wishing to end the period of revolutionary excess and in so doing to save their own skins. Tallien, Fréron, Barras, and Fouché, those who had brought down Robespierre, were opportunistic, cynical, selfish, and petty men. This was a tired age in which groups of young men with long hair and extravagant costume, known as the *Jeunesse dorée* ("gilded youth"), brawled in the streets with the surviving Jacobins. Dancing and gambling became a mania. In brief one recognizes the letdown after an almost intolerable period of emotional tension and ever-present fear.

The new leaders of France had no desire to continue the ruthless machinery of the Terror. The Committee of Public Safety was restricted to the conduct of war and diplomacy, its other great emergency powers being returned to sixteen new committees of the Convention. The Revolutionary Tribunal was reduced in power and in May 1795 abolished.

Since some of the *sections* had rallied in support of Robespierre, all members of the Paris Commune were outlawed and its duties were taken over by the Convention. The principal revolutionary legislation was repealed: the Law of Prairial, the Ventôse Decrees, the Law of Suspects, and the Great Law of the Maximum. In November the Paris Jacobin Club was closed. Some further terrorists associated with extreme violence were brought to the guillotine. In the field of religion some attempts were made to maintain the civic religion of the Jacobin period. Clerical pensions, although supposedly still guaranteed by the Civil Constitution of the Clergy, were abolished and formal religious teaching was forbidden in the schools. Despite these moves a considerable revival of traditional religion was apparent, so much so that in February 1795 a decree recognizing religious liberty was issued. In its closing days the Convention formally guaranteed free worship and brought the Civil Constitution of the Clergy to an end by announcing the complete separation of Church and State.

The Thermidoreans were to make impressive advances (at least on paper) in the field of education. A series of decrees announced plans for a Conservatory of Arts and Crafts, normal schools, a Conservatory of Music, a Polytechnical School, and schools of artillery, military engineering, roads and bridges, mines, geography, naval engineering, law, natural history, medicine, and Oriental studies. The heavily technical aspect of all these plans is obvious. The Thermidoreans also created the National Institute to honor France's most distinguished scholars, reorganized the old Royal Library as the National Library, converted the Louvre into a museum, and set up the National Archives. The earlier years of the Revolution had seen several important statements of policy in the field of public education. One of the last acts of the Convention was to continue in this direction. The decree of October 25, 1795, provided for one or more elementary schools in each canton to teach "reading, writing, arithmetic, and the elements of public morality." Each department was to have at least one central, or secondary, school, and further special schools, including those for the deaf and blind, were to be established. The framework now existed for a comprehensive educational structure covering all levels.

No more than their predecessors could the Thermidoreans escape the continued pressure of economic hardships as official controls were removed and prices rose. Bread, which had once been held at a price of twelve sous for the four-pound loaf, rose to twenty-five sous in March and to sixty-five sous in April. Demonstrations outside bakers' shops were followed in April by a mass invasion of the Convention by men and women demanding "bread and the Constitution of 1793." Since emergency measures to meet the shortages were inadequate, in May even larger crowds, supported by armed groups of the National Guard, threatened the Tuileries. The disturbances lasted two days, with the consequence that in one of the Revolution's largest displays of military force the Convention was obliged to assemble forty thousand troops to restore order. These two revolts of Germinal and Prairial, both failures, marked the last two great *sans-culotte* demonstrations of the Revolution.

The Thermidoreans were able to continue the successes in foreign affairs begun by their predecessors. A royalist landing at Quiberon Bay in Brittany, supported by British naval forces, was repulsed in June 1795. More significant was the progress in the main battle areas of the war. By the close of 1794 both the Austrian Netherlands and the Rhineland were fully occupied, Holland was soon after invaded and the Pyrenees slopes cleared of Spanish troops. What most Frenchmen now accepted as the "natural frontiers" had been won. After secret negotiations in Switzerland, Prussia signed the Peace of Basel (April 1795) conceding to France the Prussian territories on the left bank of the Rhine. In May, by the Treaty of The Hague, Holland ceded the Rhenish frontier areas of Dutch Flanders, Maestricht, and Venloo. In another Peace of Basel (July), Spain ceded its half of the island of Santo Domingo to France. Since other states also soon abandoned the Coalition, England and Austria alone remained at war with a France that had triumphed over what once seemed impossible obstacles.

Amid these dramatic and melodramatic events the Convention could now remind itself that its original purpose, to create a constitution for a republican France, still remained unachieved. Since clearly the ultrademocratic Constitution of 1793 could not now be put into effect a new document known as the Constitution of the Year III (1795) was drafted. It was to remain in effect for more than four years.

This third written constitution in four years began with a cautious Declaration of Rights, reaffirming the sanctity of property and including also a list of duties. Property qualifications restricted the number of voters; deputies were chosen by a two-stage process of election and were to be substantial property owners and at least thirty years old. The legislature was to consist of two chambers. First, a body of 750 would be elected; it would then select from its membership 250 members, at least forty years old, to make up the Council of Ancients. By a possibly unique provision, these latter had to be either married or widowers. The lower house, the Council of Five Hundred, was to initiate and discuss legislation; the Council of Ancients gave the final approval. Each house was to be renewed by one-third annually.

Executive power lay in the hands of five directors chosen by the Ancients from lists prepared by the Five Hundred. The directors acted as

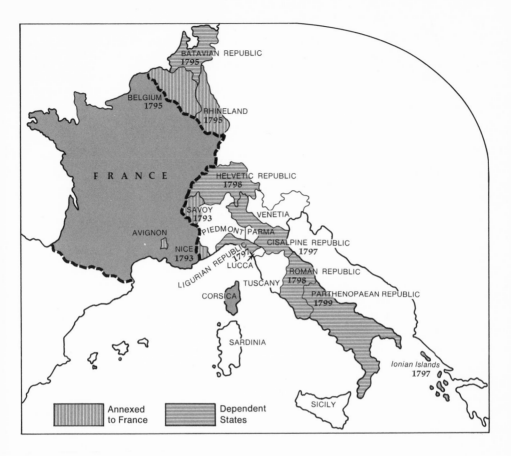

FRENCH EXPANSION, 1793–1799

Gains shown in this map are dramatically greater than those made by
Louis XIV. Republican annexations won France the "natural frontiers," while
the areas under French control by 1799 went far beyond them. The papal
territory of Avignon had been annexed in 1791.

a board; they had control of the ministries; they were not responsible to the legislative branch; and one of them, chosen by lot, was to be replaced annually. The basic administrative machinery as well as the judicial and the financial provisions established under the Constitution of 1791 remained substantially unaltered. It is clear that this new constitution, perhaps somewhat excessively maligned by its critics, was intended by its elaborate system of checks and balances to prevent any radical assumption of power by a single group or party. At the last minute the members of the Convention voted a supplementary decree to the effect that two-thirds of the membership in the new legislative bodies must be drawn from the existing membership of the Convention. This provoked the last great public demonstration of the Revolution, though it differed notably from its predecessors. The crowds who gathered in Vendémiaire (October 1795) were egged on by secret royalists and by financial conservatives who did not wish to see the Convention perpetuate any part of itself. They made use of the economic situation in order to play for the support of the *sans-culottes*—a support which they did not get. Yet from other sources they were able to muster substantial crowds and it was these that the Convention had to master. It did so by giving military command to Barras, who it turn gave the command of artillery to the young officer whom he had noted in action at the siege of Toulon in 1793. This Napoleon Bonaparte demonstrated his military talents so expertly that a few cannon blasts on the Rue Saint-Honoré and at the Tuileries served to disperse the crowds. The Constitution of the Year III had been saved by the most ruthless display of armed might, and the Directory thus launched could now pursue its four-year course.

5

THE DIRECTORY AND
THE TRIUMPH
OF BONAPARTE
1795–1799

Political Struggles
within the Directory

The system of government called the Directory was in effect from 1795 to 1799. It took its name from the board of five directors who wielded executive authority, and its constitution, like that of the limited monarchy of 1791, was hopefully expected to give permanence to the political structure of France. Much maligned because of the general mediocrity of its leaders and because of its ultimate failure, the Directory has retained its interest largely because it has been regarded as a period of recuperation after violent revolution, and because it provided the background for the rise of Bonaparte, the only figure in French history who can share with Louis XIV the distinction of having given his name to an age. Yet on balance the Directory had a substantial record of achievement, both in perpetuating the essential work of the revolutionary years which preceded and in providing the basic governmental forms which Bonaparte after his coup of 1799 was to amend and reinvigorate but emphatically not to destroy.

The government of France in 1795 was still "revolutionary." Although the elections did not produce, as stipulated, the necessary two-thirds drawn from the membership of the expiring Convention, this failure was quickly remedied by the process of cooptation. Three of the five directors chosen by the two elected councils were former Jacobins;

THE COUP OF BRUMAIRE, NOVEMBER 1799 *This contemporary and somewhat imaginative print shows at the right Bonaparte in the Orangerie at Saint-Cloud being assailed by deputies of the Council of Five Hundred holding daggers. He is defended by his grenadiers. At the left his brother Lucien attempts to maintain order.*

all five were regicides, that is, they had voted for the execution of Louis XVI. It has been calculated [1] that of the 750 members of the two councils over two-fifths were unhesitatingly republican, one-fifth were at heart royalists, though of a moderate complexion, and that the remainder fell somewhere in between, accepting the constitution, but having no clearly defined political allegiance.

The first five directors were hardly as bad as they have often been painted. Barras, to be sure, was a dissipated scoundrel, even if not without ability, who had first supported Robespierre, next helped to destroy him, and then went on to accumulate a large fortune under the Directory and live a life of ostentatious scandal. Whatever his failings, he was the only one of the five original directors to be still in office when the period closed. The other four (La Revellière-Lépeaux, Reubell, Letourneur, and Carnot) were reasonably capable, as were the six men whom they appointed to head the ministries. The constitution had provided that the directors wear the magnificent plumed hats and velvet costumes designed for them by the painter David who also designed the classical red togas worn by the members of the two councils. The Council of Ancients sat in the handsomely refurbished theater of the Tuileries; the Council of Five Hundred was quickly installed among the splendors of the Palais Bourbon, today the Chamber of Deputies, across the Seine.

The problems facing the Directory in 1795 were of the sort which arise in a country that has experienced the throes of violent revolution. People still lived in an atmosphere of fear, and for the majority daily life was hard. The repeal by the Thermidoreans of the various economic controls authorized in 1793 and 1794 meant that living became increasingly expensive. The cities were sadly run down, brigands infested the highways, and in some parts of France a state of actual civil war still existed. The new leaders of France commanded little respect. A consequence was that much discontent was manifested by unrepentant remnants of the extreme Jacobins at one pole and by equally unrepentant royalists at the other. The outward marks were those of a cynical and corrupt society in which wartime profiteering had become rampant and wealth was flaunted in drawing rooms, dance halls, gambling casinos, and public places. The fashionable new class of *merveilleuses* and *incroyables* wore fantastic costumes and lisped an affected speech from which consonants were almost entirely lacking. The reigning queen was Madame Tallien, known blasphemously at this time as "Our Lady of Thermidor." She and others like her moved in the circle of Barras and similar leaders who enjoyed to the full the ostentatious pleasures of these profitable

[1] By Lefebvre.

years. Nevertheless, the majority of Frenchmen still responded loyally if not with alacrity to the call to the colors; for the most part they lived respectable lives both in the country and in the cities. A good harvest in 1796 helped; some important advances were made in the manufacture of textiles, as well as in munitions; and by 1798 exports which had fallen behind imports in the two preceding years once more regained their lead.

The major domestic problem of the Directory was to maintain the stability of a republican state of which the overwhelming majority of those actually voting in the plebiscite of 1795 had in fact approved. By 1796 General Hoche succeeded in putting down royalist disorders in the western area of Vendée. This victory did not mean that the royalist threat was at an end, for the elections of 1797 renewed one-third of the membership of the two councils and resulted in a preponderantly con-servative membership. The newly chosen director, Barthélemy, leaned in the royalist direction as did Carnot, while the new president of the Council of Five Hundred, General Pichegru, was widely known to favor a royalist restoration. When the directors ordered republican clubs closed and two measures were passed repealing the severe laws against relatives of *émigrés* and against refractory clergy, a crisis was clearly at hand.

The first of the four coups of the Directorial period followed. The three republican directors wrote secretly to Bonaparte, now commanding the Army of Italy, asking for his support. They announced the discovery of a royalist plot. Bonaparte decided not to intervene himself, sending instead the bloodthirsty general Augereau, whom the directors put in command (unconstitutionally) of thirty thousand troops stationed in or near Paris. On September 3 (17 Fructidor) Barthélemy and Pichegru were arrested, while Carnot escaped in the nick of time through a back gate of the Luxembourg. The three remaining directors annulled the recent election of 198 deputies; about one-third of these were ordered deported; and military tribunals throughout France sentenced 160 sus-pects to death. A severe press censorship was enforced and the former laws against *émigrés* and recalcitrant clergy were reintroduced. Since no elections were held to fill the vacant seats in the legislature, the republi-can majority in the two chambers had been saved. Nevertheless, in Lefebvre's words, the Coup of Fructidor brought to an end the liberal experiment of the Thermidoreans and forcibly established a dictatorship; but it did not organize it. Though Bonaparte had been brought close to intervention, in the end he chose to keep out, not wishing, as he wrote, to engage in "a war of chamber-pots." Clearly, the signs for the future were ominous.

A year later, by the Coup of Floréal (May 1798), the directors struck in the opposite direction. The elections of that year had produced a large number of radical republicans, and since there had been much confusion in the procedure of the electoral assemblies the directors quickly took the drastic step of having the choice of 106 deputies annulled, replacing them by 53 "safe" governmental candidates and leaving the other seats vacant. In this way the creaking governmental machinery was given another lease on life. Still another crisis came in the summer of 1799 when new elections again recorded the triumph of radical deputies. The legislature was now strong enough to void the recent election of one director and force the resignation of two others. Their replacements, Gohier, Ducos, and Moulins, though certainly not strong men, were generally in sympathy with the popular branch.[2] The common feature of all three coups was the repeated use of highly dubious political techniques and at times armed force in place of normal constitutional procedures.

Economic and Social Reconstruction

The positive domestic work of the Directory must be set against this picture of internal coups and the growing likelihood of military intervention. From its predecessors, the Thermidoreans, it had inherited a social and economic situation which could easily lead to disaster. It is clear that despite the savagely critical picture of these years presented by historians such as Vandal and Madelin, much substantial work was nevertheless done.

The establishment of an orderly economy required the use of force to put down any opposition to the regime. Hoche had successfully subdued the royalists in Vendée by the spring of 1796, and further disturbances in southern cities were effectively handled in the autumn of 1797. On the other hand brigandage, which was deliberately encouraged by some royalists, was an irritating and continuing problem for which no solution could be found. As early as 1796 a plot against the regime was unearthed. This was Babeuf's "Conspiracy of the Equals" which has assumed a larger importance retrospectively than it probably deserved. The leader, who had assumed the fine Roman republican name of Gracchus, was an obscure land surveyor steeped in the writings of the philosophes who dreamed of a communally organized society existing without private property and with a living guaranteed to all. In and out of prison during the Revolution, Babeuf founded a paper, wrote inflam-

---

[2] This is known as the Coup of Prairial, though it resembles more closely the action of Thermidor when Robespierre and his fellows had been eliminated.

matory pamphlets, and at the Club of the Panthéon secretly gathered a small group hoping by violent means to revive the democratic Constitution of 1793. This conspiracy was discovered by the police; Babeuf and others were first shadowed and then arrested, and in 1797 he and one companion were sent to the guillotine. The conspiracy was surely a minor flash in the pan, yet "Babouvisme" has been hailed by later generations of socialists as the first militantly class-conscious effort in modern times on behalf of the proletariat.

As the guillotine fell into disuse, what was called the dry guillotine, that is, deportation to overseas prison colonies, succeeded it. In addition, a growing policy of censorship was applied to the press, with many papers suspended and some editors arrested. Laws against refractory priests and *émigrés* and their relatives remained in effect. After the Coup of Fructidor over nine thousand priests in the Belgian departments were sentenced to deportation, though actually only a very few were sent overseas. In France nearly eighteen hundred priests were similarly sentenced, though here again few of the sentences were in fact enforced.

Freedom of religion and the complete separation of Church and State had been decreed in the last months of the Convention. The purpose of the leaders of the Directory was to keep alive the various republican festivals and to encourage the exercise of civic religion. They were not too successful, for most Frenchmen were tired of such public celebrations and understandably preferred one day's rest in seven to one in ten, as the republican calendar required. A marked feature of the period, indeed, was the reopening of some churches and the gradual revival of interest in the Roman Catholic faith.

The need for economic order meant that a hands-off policy was impossible. In general the state tempered the practice of laissez-faire with a substantial degree of intervention so as to create some measure of what could be called a national economy. A most urgent problem was that of the assignats, of which billions were in circulation at about 1 percent of their face value. In 1796 they were ordered to be exchanged at about one-thirtieth of their face value for a new type of paper money, the *mandats térritoriaux*, these to be used only for the purchase of national property. Since they also deteriorated, forty billion francs worth of the new paper was repudiated in 1797 and a return made to a metallic currency.[3] Another and seemingly insoluble problem was that of the national debt. In September 1797 the Law of the Consolidated Third consolidated one-third of the national debt and required all bondholders to accept new bonds for the remaining two-thirds. These latter quickly declined

---

[3] In April 1795 the franc had replaced the livre as the basic monetary unit.

and within four years became valueless. Government solvency was thus assured, though at a very heavy cost to the public.

Taxes were also a perennial challenge. Efforts were made to increase efficiency in tax collection, and new taxes were authorized on playing cards, hackney carriages, legal documents, and even on doors and windows. Indirect taxes were also increased, a high general tariff was established, and subsidies were paid to manufacturers and inventors. Measures were passed to control foreign exchange and the operation of the stock market. A true stability had not been achieved, yet the beginnings were present. In sum, the economic work of the Directory was such as to avoid any calamitous breakdown and on the positive side to encourage the further transfer of land into bourgeois possession. Encouragement was given to industry sometimes by a hands-off policy and sometimes even by subsidies. The outlines of the typical bourgeois state of the nineteenth century were emerging, to be aided soon by the powerful hand of Napoleon.

Important steps were also taken in the field of military conscription, for the hopes of general peace had proven illusory. In September 1798 compulsory military service for all men between the ages of twenty and twenty-five was decreed; conscripts from the five classes, beginning with the youngest, were to be called up annually to meet the deficits in voluntary enlistments. Such a measure at last created order out of the old *levée en masse* introduced in the critical days of 1793.

Striking measures were taken in the field of science. In August 1793 the Convention had decreed the introduction of the metric system, with the gram and the meter as the basic units. Between July and December 1799 amid the confusions attending Bonaparte's seizure of power, the system both with respect to currency and weights and measures was elaborated and precisely defined. The Institute of France, founded by a decree of the Convention in October 1795, had a thriving existence all through this period. French mathematicians such as Monge, Fourier, Lagrange, and above all Laplace (whose monumental *Mécanique céleste* began to appear in 1799), as well as great chemists such as Berthollet, students of natural history such as Cuvier, Lamarck, and Geoffroy Saint-Hilaire, the philosopher-linguist Volney, and the learned legal scholar Daunou would have given distinction to any age.[4] When Bonaparte, just elected to the Institute, embarked on his expedition to Egypt in 1798 he took with him a distinguished group of scholars to survey that ancient land, among them Monge, Berthollet, Fourier, Saint-Hilaire, and the

---

[4] The great chemist Lavoisier had been guillotined in 1794 after the notorious statement at his trial that "the Republic has no need of scientists."

artist Denon. Even that brilliant woman of letters Madame de Staël, later the implacable foe of Napoleon, found much to admire in the Directorial period. Along with such vigorous intellectual activity went the gradual establishment of the technical institutes earlier authorized by the Convention.

In still another area a commission set up in 1796 produced the *Plan des Artistes*, a magnificent seventy-two page atlas having among its proposals a symmetrical system of main streets in Paris radiating from the Place Vendôme, an enlargement of the *quais* along the Seine, and an extension of the Champs Elysées all the way to the bridge at Neuilly. Though not much of this was achieved, the Luxembourg Palace was refurbished for the directors and the fine classical hall was prepared for the Council of Five Hundred in the Palais Bourbon. This, with the parallel activity in the learned fields, is a remarkable commentary upon the vitality of French life amid the exhausting years of what was still a revolutionary age.

The Fortunes of War

The significance of the years 1795–1799 in French foreign policy was enormous, for during them France advanced from the program of natural frontiers to one of active intervention beyond them. This new role meant, first, the creation of a chain of sister republics all the way from the North Sea to southern Italy and the establishment within them of political institutions closely resembling those of Directorial France. Although these new republics were based ostensibly on representative assemblies, they were in fact subject to French control from above. More than once military force or the threat of force was used to bring about desired changes—a significant portent for the military coup of 1799 in France itself. In the second place, France was committed to a policy of major war, which with some brief interruptions was to go on until 1815. Finally, the close of the period was to bring a young revolutionary general, Napoleon Bonaparte, to a commanding position in France and very soon also in Europe.

Bonaparte had achieved a modest distinction as an artillery officer during the Revolution. Shortly after his success on the day of Vendémiaire (October 5, 1795) he had met, wooed, and won Josephine Beauharnais, an attractive widow born in Martinique whose husband, a former nobleman, had been sent to the guillotine in 1794; because of the confusions following the fall of Robespierre she herself narrowly missed this fate. Six years older than Bonaparte, she was one of the gay ladies living by their wits whom Barras delighted to have around him in his seraglio at the Luxembourg. In 1796 the directors were planning a two-pronged campaign against Austria involving an advance across the Rhine into south Germany and another in northern Italy. Bonaparte's appointment to the Italian command at the age of twenty-six was chiefly the decision of Carnot, the director responsible for military affairs, who had observed the young soldier's brilliant work in the army's topographical bureau at Paris. In March 1796, two days after his wedding, Bonaparte left Paris for his momentous rendezvous with destiny.

The Italian campaign of 1796–1797 established Bonaparte as one of the great masters of the art of war. His youthful training as an artillery officer had exposed him to the work of the leading military theorists of the *ancien régime*, men as important in their way as the philosophes were in theirs. Breaking away from the formal parade-ground tactics of eighteenth-century war, a number of French military writers had successfully imposed their ideas upon the army. Du Teil's *Use of the New Artillery in Open War* stressed the employment of massed artillery to support infantry at decisive moments. Bourcet's *Principles of Mountain Warfare* advocated the technique of wide dispersal in order to move and quick concentration in order to fight. Two books by the famous Guibert, *A General Essay on Tactics* and *A Defense of Modern Warfare*, were prophetic. Mobility was all important, Guibert taught; armies must live off the land, and ideally in order to guarantee high morale they should be citizen armies. In the great dispute over the respective advantages of column and line formation Guibert stressed the "mixed order"—columns for approach, and a combination of column and line at the last moment for attack. Weapons used during the Revolution were essentially those of the *ancien régime*. The smoothbore musket standardized in 1777 remained in use until 1840, and the lighter weight cannon designed by Gribeauval in the 1760s remained unchanged until 1825. Bonaparte's particular genius lay in the masterful carrying out of these theories ("everything is in the execution"), in his dramatic use of showmanship and propaganda, and in his keen perception of the political necessities associated with actual warfare.

The first purpose of the Italian campaign was to separate and defeat Austria's ally, Savoy. This was done within a month. Bonaparte then advanced across the Lombard plain, winning a notable battle at the bridge of Lodi; by mid-May he entered the great north Italian city of Milan. Next the kingdom of Naples was driven out of the war and armistices were made with Tuscany and the Papal States. Further victories at Castiglione, Bassano, Arcola, and Rivoli in the last half of 1796 gave Bonaparte a dominant position aganist the Austrians. In February 1797 the great fortress of Mantua guarding the mountain approaches to Austrian territory fell, and by April Bonaparte had pushed beyond the head of the Adriatic and was high in the Julian Alps, less than one hundred miles from Vienna, where panic understandably reigned.

In this intoxicating atmosphere of military victory, other notable changes were in the making. One was in the field of revenues, for war was doing more than simply paying its way. As early as May 1796 Bonaparte was able to report to the Directory that bullion valued at millions was on its way to France. Art treasures were ruthlessly confiscated, and by the formal Treaty of Tolentino with the papacy in February 1797 payments of thirty million livres as well as long lists of priceless art objects were stipulated. The Directory could hardly quarrel with a victorious general thus easing its crushing financial burdens.

The other aspect of war was territorial. The Treaty of Tolentino obliged the papacy to recognize the annexation of Avignon by France. More significantly, changes were also being made outside the French frontiers. As early as January 1795, following the French invasion, the Convention had created the Batavian Republic out of the former territory of the Netherlands. The Republic, with "Liberty, Equality, and Fraternity" as its motto, had allied itself with France, and had agreed to pay an indemnity of a hundred million florins. The first of the Italian sister republics emerged in October 1796, when Bonaparte created the Cispadane Republic out of the papal territories of Modena, Bologna, and Ferrara. In June 1797 Genoese territories were reorganized into a new Ligurian Republic. Then between July and October of that year Bonaparte's most brilliant creation, the Cisalpine Republic, was made by adding the former Austrian provinces north of the River Po to the Cispadane Republic, with Milan as its capital. (See map, p. 75)

All these Italian republics were given institutions similar to those of the Directory in France, with the addition of a strong French controlling hand, and all were required to contribute heavily to the French treasury. After Bonaparte left Italy, disorders in Rome caused the pope to flee his territories, with the consequence that still another sister, the Roman Republic, was proclaimed in 1798. Even later, when the king of Naples sought to restore the pope, his mainland territories were occupied in 1799 and converted into the Neapolitan Republic. A popular revolt in the Swiss cantons led to a similar French intervention and to the proclamation (March 1798) of the Helvetic Republic, allied to France and with a constitution inspired by that of the Directory.

Along with such territorial changes went a long series of armistices and peace treaties: with Savoy, with the papacy, and to the north with

Württemberg, Baden, and Bavaria, these all having sided with Austria. Even Britain, the hitherto implacable foe of the French Revolution, undertook peace negotiations at Paris in 1796 and again at Lille in the summer of 1797, though the French insistence on large colonial cessions, along with other disagreements, caused negotiations to be broken off in September. The great triumph, however, was the settlement which the victorious Bonaparte was able to make with Austria. The spectacular advance of the French Army of Italy towards Vienna caused the Austrians in April 1797 to accept an armistice at Leoben. Throughout the summer Bonaparte, largely ignoring the instructions sent him by the Directory and living in semiroyal state at his headquarters, worked out his own definitive peace terms.

The outcome was the Peace of Campo Formio, signed in October, by which Austria withdrew from the war, recognized the Cisalpine Republic, ceded the Austrian Netherlands (Belgium) to France, and agreed in a secret article to support French claims to the entire left bank area of the Rhine in a forthcoming congress to be held at Rastatt. Three other points were significant. The thousand-year-old Venetian Republic, which included both a large land territory in northern Italy and areas stretching far down the east coast of the Adriatic, was destroyed, most of it going to Austria as compensation for its losses in Lombardy, Belgium, and the Rhineland. Austria was also promised support in gaining the great archbishopric of Salzburg, a rich area touching its borders. Bonaparte used some of Venice's mainland areas to round out the Cisalpine Republic and in addition he secured the Ionian Islands, a strategic group of seven islands off the west coast of Greece which in the possession of France were a clue to Bonaparte's as yet concealed ambitions for a dramatic advance into the Near East. (See map, p. 75) Though the twenty-seven-year-old Bonaparte was not as yet master of France, he was pushing his country (and himself) at top speed into a European role of unprecedented power. Understandably, when he returned to Paris in December 1797, he was greeted as a hero. All this, it should be noted, had been done at a time when the advance of the French into south Germany had proved a humiliating failure.

Only Britain now remained in the war. A quick inspection of the Channel coast led Bonaparte to report to the directors that an invasion of England was not at that time feasible. He had been closely concerned with political developments in France at the time of the 1797 Coup of Fructidor. Some deputies, indeed, had denounced him for his ruthless destruction of the Venetian Republic. Hence his ambitions now shrewdly turned in other directions. Here lay the genesis of his next spectacular adventure, the Egyptian expedition.

French interests in the Near East went back to the time of the Crusades and had been periodically renewed. A new intervention would both secure and enlarge those ancient interests, would seriously damage Britain's trade with the Levant, and would open a new route perhaps even to India, where France still held a few trading posts. Supported by Talleyrand, Bonaparte won the approval of the directors. The outcome was the departure from Toulon in May 1798 of a convoy of 400 transports carrying an army of 38,000 troops and also a body of some 150 distinguished antiquarians, geologists, naturalists, and mathematicians, as has been indicated earlier, to study the wonders of these ancient lands. En route the French occupied the island of Malta, small but of enormous strategic importance and governed by the Knights of St. John, the weak survivors of a once famous crusading Order whose protector in 1796 became the new Tsar Paul of Russia.

The first landings at Alexandria were so successful that Bonaparte was able to win the Battle of the Pyramids against native forces. Two events changed the picture. The British naval commander, Lord Nelson, found the French fleet anchored at Aboukir Bay, and in the Battle of the Nile (August 1798) he destroyed it. A month later the sultan, who claimed a general sovereignty over Egypt, declared war on France. To meet this new threat Bonaparte marched northward from Egypt into Syria, capturing Jaffa and besieging Acre. Lack of supplies, the ravages of typhus, and news that a Second Coalition was being formed against France ended his hopes of a brilliant victory. Bonaparte retreated to Egypt, routed a Turkish army, double the size of the French, which had been put ashore at Aboukir, and then decided that his only policy was to abandon the remnants of his troops and undertake a risky secret return, almost alone, to France. Fears of what the Second Coalition might accomplish, together with reports of the political confusions in France, reinforced his decision to abandon what had become an impossible military adventure.

The fruits of the Egyptian campaign were largely political. News of Bonaparte's recent victory over the Turks at Aboukir preceded him. Since his great losses were not appreciated, he could pose as the man of destiny in a France where hopes that he could quickly end the war in Europe were widespread. He was soon able, therefore, to take advantage of the situation which confronted him. In a very different way the expedition was a historic landmark, for it inaugurated the scientific study of Egyptian antiquities. The ten folio volumes of the *Description of Egypt* and the ten further volumes of detailed maps were the outcome of work begun by the French in 1798. The trilingual inscription found by a French officer in the little village of Rosetta made it possible ultimately to unlock the secret of Egyptian hieroglyphs. Moreover, the Egyptian motifs which were quickly popularized in furniture, interior *décor*, and architecture contributed notably to what soon was to be known as the "Empire Style"—"*le style Empire.*"

The Coup of Brumaire

The moves by which Bonaparte became political master of France at the close of 1799 were made possible by the political situation within France and by the posture of military affairs in Europe. Although on balance the Directory had a creditable record of achievement at home, the domestic atmosphere was clouded with uncertainty, while abroad the military situation early in 1799 seemed to be approaching disaster. A Second Coalition had taken shape, largely due to the efforts of William Pitt, the British prime minister, who was determined that the continental war must be renewed on a large scale. The need for such a renewal was underscored by an abortive rising in Ireland in the summer of 1798, aided by the French, which the English quickly put down.

Russia, whose interests throughout the revolutionary years had been concentrated in Eastern Europe, was the first to join the coalition, allying with the Turks in December 1798 on the promise of a free passage through the Straits, and in the same month with England and the king of Naples. Continued French intrigues in Italy led to armed skirmishes with the Austrians, the outcome being that by March 1799 Austria was again at war with France. Savoy also joined the coalition, as did Sweden, although very late (October 1799) and without making any military contributions. Even the United States, outraged at French interference with American shipping, carried on its "Undeclared War" against French commercial traffic on the high seas. Only Prussia among the major powers, satisfied at its preponderant role in northern Germany, rejected all overtures to join. Apart from the desire to make selfish gains, European governments were alarmed at French continued interference and exactions throughout all the sister republics.

The opening months of the new war went very badly for the French. An invasion of Germany by General Jourdan failed so badly that he was forced back into Alsace. In Italy the French were compelled to abandon the Neapolitan, the Roman, and the Cisalpine republics, holding little more than Genoa. These disasters were due in part to the presence for the first time in Italy of a substantial Russian army led by the famous General Suvarov in support of the Austrians. Having victoriously occupied Milan, he forced his way northward through the St. Gothard Pass into eastern Switzerland. Concurrently, a combined Anglo-Russian force made a landing on the coast of the Batavian Republic.

Such signs of impending disaster, which are often given as the reason for Bonaparte's success in overthrowing the government of the Directory, led to a number of ruthless measures in France before his return. A new *levée en masse* was ordered in June 1799, making it possible to call up all five of the annual classes of conscripts in one year. A very severe new Law of Hostages was authorized in July, and a forced loan of a hundred million francs was imposed in September. In point of fact, however, the military situation had redressed itself substantially before Bonaparte's return. Masséna's victory at Zurich in September led to the complete withdrawal of Russian forces from Switzerland and was accompanied by the gradual reassertion of French authority in Italy. The Anglo-Russian landings in the Netherlands were countered by General Brune, who forced a humiliating withdrawal upon the invaders. What France was urgently seeking in the autumn of 1799 was much less a new series of military victories than the rapid reestablishment of general peace.

The Coup of 18 and 19 Brumaire (November 9 and 10, 1799) must be ranked as one of the great coups d'état of history, for it made a victorious soldier, Bonaparte, the master of France. In one sense it was almost inevitable, for a weak Directory and a legislature of uncertain purpose had reached the point of complete deadlock. In the course of three years three lesser coups (Fructidor, Floréal and Prairial), to say nothing of at least a dozen other minor violations, had seen the constitution abused. Bonaparte's military reputation was enormous, and the true extent of his losses in Egypt still remained unknown to the public. In another sense a remarkable degree of improvisation was involved in the coup. Bonaparte had been deeply concerned at the political situation of France in 1797 at the time of the Coup of Fructidor, yet he had not then chosen to intervene directly. He had been absent in Egypt during the two coups of 1799, and there is nothing to show that he had actively sought to organize a further coup during his stay there. The first initiative, indeed, was taken by a number of figures in Paris, most notably Sieyès, Barras, Fouché, and Talleyrand, who were disillusioned with the Directorial regime and were looking for a military leader, not necessarily Bonaparte, to wield the sword when the occasion arose. Yet they had not been able to arrive at any precise plan.

Bonaparte landed near Fréjus, on the south coast of France, on October 9. Just a week later, after a triumphal progress, he was in Paris. It took less than a month for him to make his new and secret plans. He was officially received by the directors, modestly attended a session of the Institute, and was given a banquet by the legislature at the former church of Saint-Sulpice. The military situation had vastly improved, yet it might become dangerous once again, and royalism was always a threat in the western departments. The essence of the emerging conspiracy was to find a means whereby with some outward show of legality the existing government could authorize Bonaparte to remodel the creaking machinery of state. Among the five directors, Bonaparte detested Barras and was contemptuous of Sieyès as being only a theorist. Ducos was harmless enough to allow him to be kept in office. The other two men—the nonentities Gohier and Moulin—would simply have to be forced out. The conspiracy put together in haste at Bonaparte's modest house in Paris involved Talleyrand, Fouché, Cambacérès, many generals, and Lucien Bonaparte, the last now most opportunely president of the Council of Five Hundred.

Using the pretext of a Jacobin plot, those members of the Council of Ancients who were deemed trustworthy were summoned to an early morning meeting on November 9. The Council of Ancients on being told of the supposed plot voted to transfer the session for the next day to Saint-Cloud, on the outskirts of Paris (which was legal) and to appoint Bonaparte commander of the troops of Paris (which was illegal). The Council of Five Hundred, meeting in the afternoon, was simply informed of these decisions, which it had no power to alter. During the day Sieyès and Ducos by prearrangement submitted their resignations from the Directory, while Barras, under pressure, unhappily did the same. The other two directors, refusing to resign, were held under guard at the Luxembourg.

The great crisis came in the meetings of November 10 at Saint-Cloud, for then the actual transfer of power would have to be effected. Bonaparte arrived dramatically with a large contingent of troops. His first appearance before the Council of Ancients, where he announced that the Directory as a board no longer existed, encountered some hostile criticism, and worse followed when he sought to address the Council of Five Hundred. Here the protest from the Jacobin deputies was so violent that an uproar ensued, and Bonaparte was so savagely threatened and even shaken that he stammered and was dragged by the soldiers, half-fainting, from the hall. Lucien tried to save the day by a speech, then resigned his presidency, dissolved the session, and went outside to address the assembled troops, declaring that Bonaparte had been threatened with daggers, and urging the soldiers to "restore order" within. A file of grenadiers commanded by Leclerc and Murat entered the Orangerie where the Five

Hundred were sitting and at bayonet point drove them out. Many left through the windows, casting their red togas aside in the gardens as they fled into the gathering dusk.

Later in the evening some of the deputies, perhaps sixty, were unceremoniously rounded up so as to give a semblance of legality to the final proceedings. Bonaparte, Sieyès, and Ducos were recognized as three provisional consuls. With the aid of a committee of fifty drawn from both houses they were to revise the constitution. However low Sieyès may have stood in Bonaparte's opinion, he had an extraordinary fund of ideas in the realm of constitution making; moreover the presence of Sieyès and Ducos as consuls would provide a plausible link of continuity with the preceding regime. The legislature was to be adjourned for six weeks and sixty-one specified Jacobin members were formally to be excluded from it. Intrigue, combined with a ruthless show of force, had toppled not only the directors—mourned by few—but also the elected representatives of the French people.

6

NAPOLEONIC FRANCE

The Times and the Man

Few periods of history give as much opportunity as does the Napoleonic epoch to consider the interwoven phenomena of "the times" and "the man." Napoleon never failed to recognize his indebtedness to the years of revolution which preceded his assumption of power. "The French Revolution," so he dictated to Las Casas at St. Helena in 1816, "was . . . a general mass movement of the nation against the privileged classes. . . . And no matter what has been said, this memorable era will be linked to my person, because, after all, I have carried its torch and consecrated its principles, and because persecution now has made me its Messiah." [1] His administrative gifts and his mental powers were superb, his energy seemingly inexhaustible, his ruthlessness proverbial. On the other hand he could show deep emotion and sympathy when aware of the exceptional loyalty of one of his officers or private soldiers. His last letter to Josephine whom he had divorced in 1810 for reasons of state, written when he abdicated at Fontainebleau in 1814, is similar: "Never lose the memory," he begged her, "of one who has never forgotten you, and never will forget you."

Napoleon had the understandable feelings of a man of action towards men and women of mere ideas. "The metaphysicians," he declared, "are

[1] This and subsequent quotations are from J. C. Herold (ed.), *The Mind of Napoleon* (1955), *passim*.

my pet aversion." Madame de Staël he termed "an old crow." Rousseau
was "a mere chatterbox." Of Lafayette he said, "Perhaps Lafayette is right
in theory—but what is theory? Mere nonsense, if you want to apply it
to human masses." To one of his generals in 1799 he wrote: "If you wage
war, do it energetically and with severity. This is the only way to make
it shorter, and consequently less inhuman." To Berthier he wrote in 1808,
"War justifies everything."

Napoleon was confident that he had a destiny in France and in Europe
to destroy outworn institutions and create new. "A consecutive series of
great actions," he told Las Casas, "never is the result of chance and luck;
it always is the product of planning and genius." Even so, it is not always
easy to make his professed intentions tally with his actions. In 1807 he
wrote to his brother Jerome, then king of Westphalia, as follows: "The
peoples of Germany, the people of France, of Italy, of Spain all desire
equality and liberal ideas. I have guided the affairs of Europe for many
years now, and I have had occasion to convince myself that the buzzing
of the privileged classes is contrary to the general opinion. Be a constitutional king." How far his actions were consistent with these fine professions the following pages will show. As for the cost to himself, he had as
a young officer written prophetically in one of his private notebooks of
1791: "Men of genius are meteors, destined to be consumed in lighting
up their century."

Consular France: The Framework

During the period of a little more than four years known as the Consulate
Bonaparte exerted his remarkable talents in every sphere of activity.
In November 1799 Sieyès and his fellow Brumairians had hoped to
crush the existing Directorial leaders, using the strong sword of General Bonaparte to this end. They were hardly prepared for the immediate
sequel to their first victory, for in the ensuing month of December what
might well be called the Coup of Frimaire drove most of the conspirators
of Brumaire into the shadows and left Bonaparte the unchallenged master of France. By a series of bold strokes he went on to push aside the
constitutional planning of Sieyès, forced through a strikingly effective
scheme of government, brought about order at home and peace abroad,
and followed these achievements with a wide program of domestic reforms destined to leave their indelible mark upon France. The clue to
all that he undertook is found in the two words, order and authority.

The constitution was the first problem, and here Bonaparte quickly
disposed of Sieyès's scheme. This would have elevated the victorious
general to the dubious and shadowy role of "Grand Elector," leaving

the actual work of government to two consuls and to a legislature chosen indirectly on the basis of universal manhood suffrage. In his work of constitution making Bonaparte was ably supported by Benjamin Constant and Pierre Daunou, both theorists of genuine ability. The outcome, proclaimed late in December 1799, was the Constitution of the Year VIII—France's fourth written constitution in a decade.

The constitution did not bother with a bill of rights. Though all Frenchmen over twenty-one could vote, their actual power was minimal. Citizens in each locality drew up a communal list of one-tenth of their number from which local officials were to be appointed. Members of the communal lists selected one-tenth of their number to compose the departmental lists, and these in turn chose the national list—the notables of France. This process of reduction meant that in the end about six thousand names remained from whom the members of the two legislative bodies and holders of high administrative positions would be selected.[2]

A Council of State, appointed by the first consul, would draft and initiate legislation under his direction. A Conservative Senate (*Sénat conservateur*) made up of eighty life members, most of whom were originally chosen by the three consuls, was principally concerned with selecting from the national list members of the two legislative bodies. These comprised a Tribunate of one hundred members chosen for five-year terms, which discussed but did not vote the laws, and a Legislative Body of 300, similarly chosen, with the duty of voting but not discussing. Their conclusions were to be returned to the Council of State and then, if satisfactory, promulgated by the consuls.

All this machinery was kept from turning into an organized paralysis by the driving force of the first consul working through the Council of State. The three consuls, who were named in the constitution, were to serve for ten years. Bonaparte was named first consul, with Cambacérès, a distinguished jurist, and Lebrun, the translator of Tasso and Homer, as his colleagues. Sieyès became president of the Senate. The first consul appointed the heads of the seven ministries, all ambassadors, high military officers, prefects of the departments, and upper magistrates. Since Bonaparte dominated the selection of the members both of the Council of State and the Senate, in the latter of whose hands the selection of members for the two legislative bodies largely lay, and since the duties of the second and third consuls were merely consultative, his was incontestably the dominating will. Work on the constitution, whipped along

---

[2] One reaches this figure by starting with 6,000,000 eligible local voters, reduced to 600,000 in the communal lists, then to 60,000 in the departmental lists, then to 6,000 in the national list.

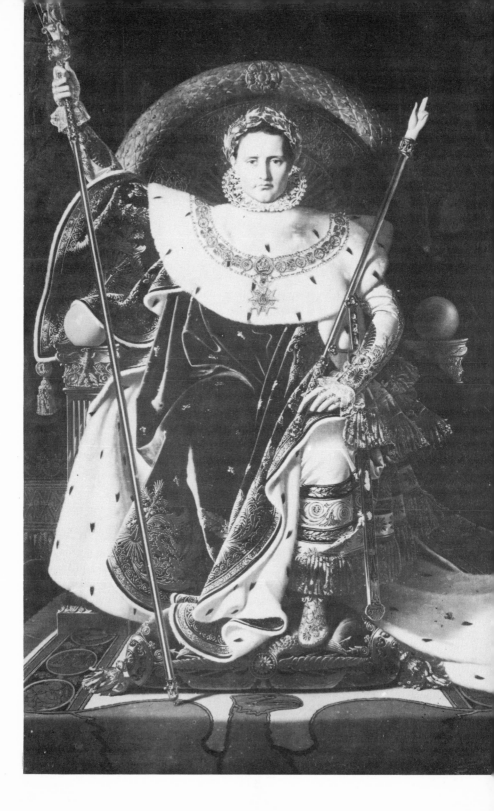

by Bonaparte, was completed in a month. A plebiscite, completed in February 1800 produced three million votes in its favor and only fifteen hundred against.

Local government felt the same strong hand. The departments, which now numbered ninety, to which nine external departments in Belgium and Luxembourg were added, remained as one of the great constructive achievements of the Revolution. Prefects, subprefects, major police officers, and mayors were now appointed by the first consul. It has been noted perceptively by Tocqueville that these prefects were in fact a new version of the intendants of the *ancien régime*. The various administrative councils assisting them were elected for very long periods, either of fifteen or twenty years. The system of law courts arising from the earlier work of the Revolution was also retained, with some modifications, and all judges save the local justices of the peace were appointed from Paris. Popular election and true local self-government were thus now largely at an end, replaced by a characteristically Napoleonic centralization of authority.

All this very rapid initial work was accomplished at a time when the public was clamoring for peace. Although the military situation had improved dramatically by the eve of Brumaire, the Italian scene soon worsened again to the point of possible disaster. Bonaparte's letters on Christmas Day 1799 to George III of England and the Emperor Francis of Austria urging peace negotiations were both rebuffed. Fortunately, the renewed royalist disturbances in Vendée were soon put down by General Brune with forty thousand troops, and Bonaparte urged the several royalist leaders who were bold enough to approach him to forget their dreams and accept the new consular regime. He could point out that the repressive Law of Hostages had been repealed, that many royalist names were being removed from the long proscription lists earlier drawn up by the police, and that freedom of worship had been guaranteed. When the future Louis XVIII, brother of Louis XVI, wrote from Warsaw asking Bonaparte to help in a Bourbon restoration, he received a crushing reply: "You must no longer look forward to your return to France. Your path would assuredly lie over one hundred thousand corpses."

Although order was reasonably restored at home, the military danger abroad remained. The Mediterranean situation was unsure, for the British, who threatened both Egypt and Malta, were also blockading Genoa, while the Ionian Islands conceded to France in 1797 had been set up as a republic under Russian protection. The new French plans were four-

◀ NAPOLEON AS EMPEROR, 1804, BY INGRES *The painting from the Museum of the Invalides shows Napoleon in coronation robes of oriental splendor wearing the Grand Cross of the Legion of Honor.*

fold: naval activity was to be renewed in the Mediterranean; Moreau was to lead an army across the Rhine against the Austrians; Masséna was to command another army in Piedmont: and Berthier was given the command of a reserve army assembling at Díjon and intended to move secretly through Switzerland and across the Great St. Bernard Pass into Italy. Although as first consul Bonaparte could not properly assume command in the field, he nevertheless went to Switzerland, whence in one of his most spectacular moves he led forty thousand men across the snow-packed mule paths of the Great St. Bernard into Italy. Reoccupying Milan, he met the Austrians at Marengo on June 14 and was in the end victorious after a nip-and-tuck battle—certainly not masterly in execution but profoundly important in its fortunate outcome. The war, however, was not yet over, for Genoa surrendered to the Austrians, and other fighting continued. The decisive stroke came in December 1800, when Moreau's army won the victory of Hohenlinden against the Austrians near Munich and then advanced to within fifty miles of Vienna.

Negotiations with Austria quickly led to the Peace of Lunéville, signed in February 1801. This was in general a repetition of the Peace of Campo Formio. Austria now formally recognized the cession of all the left bank of the Rhine to France and the existence of the sister republics. A month before the treaty Bonaparte had been elected president of the Cisalpine. The French were formally authorized to take the lead in the arrangements by which those German princes dispossessed in the Rhineland would be compensated for their losses by new lands within Germany. With reason, German historians have never failed to single this out as a classic example of the fateful French determination to meddle in affairs across the Rhine.

The full breakup of the Second Coalition quickly followed. Tsar Paul of Russia, furious at the British seizure of Malta in September 1800, persuaded Sweden, Denmark, and Prussia to form a League of Armed Neutrality to oppose British interference with neutral shipping. When Paul was assassinated in a palace plot, his son and successor, Alexander I, quickly made peace (October, 1801) with France. Spain withdrew from the war in March 1801, ceding Louisiana to France in return for Tuscany, which was to go to the Spanish king's son-in-law. When Naples, Portugal, and Turkey also made peace, England alone was left in the war.

The atmosphere for negotiation became more favorable when in February 1801 William Pitt was forced out of office and the second-rate Addington succeeded him as prime minister. Trade had suffered through the closing of the continental markets and England was war-weary. Protracted negotiations finally led to the Peace of Amiens in March 1802. Britain recognized the French Republic, keeping only Ceylon and Trinidad out of its colonial conquests from the French and Dutch. It returned the Cape of Good Hope to the Dutch and gave Egypt (which it had occupied) back to the sultan. England also promised to give up Malta. Bonaparte had achieved the general peace which all France had desired and had moreover won an impressive European position. Britain had accepted French control both of the Rhineland and of northern Italy. Talleyrand, reflecting upon this situation, wrote in his *Memoirs*: "France had climbed from the depths of degradation into which the Directory had plunged it to the leading position in Europe." The verdict was to a large degree just.

Consular France:
The Domestic Achievement

Under the Consulate the great work of domestic reform could now forge ahead. Financial problems which, as always, remained pressing were met not by any dramatic panaceas but by a determined effort at order and efficiency. In Bonaparte's view, little financial discretion could be granted, as had been the case before, to local authorities; policy would be fixed at Paris, the prefects would receive their orders, and a corps of professionally trained local officials would then move into action. The able minister of finance, Gaudin, deserves much of the credit for the operation of a smoothly working financial machine. Government indebtedness was heavy. The bonds known as the Consolidated Third, which had been created in 1797 when two-thirds of the government debt was repudiated, had fallen to 7 percent of their face value in 1799. By 1800 they had returned to 44 percent, and in 1802 they rose to 53 percent. A special bank, the *Caisse d'amortissement* was set up to guarantee the 5 percent interest due to bondholders and to purchase bonds on the bourse when their price threatened to drop too suddenly. The Bank of France, created in 1800, though theoretically a private institution with several hundred shareholders and fifteen elected regents, was in fact government dominated, with the exclusive right to issue bank notes. In 1803 a new silver and gold coinage was issued according to the metric basis earlier established. For the financial year 1801–1802 the budget was declared to be in balance, though because of deceptive bookkeeping and the ruthless insistence upon subsidies from the tributary republics this balance was to a large degree illusory. Some industrial growth resulted; to encourage this the first consul was tireless in the visits he paid to new manufacturing establishments and in pushing for what were in general mildly mercantilist policies embodying encouragement rather than actual direction.

Still another pressing need in the great cause of an orderly society was to continue the legal reforms which had had their beginnings in the days of the Constituent Assembly. A committee set up in 1800 completed the first draft of a new Civil Code by December. Though pushed hard by the first consul who, though no legal expert, had a powerfully lucid mind and tireless energies, this code was not formally proclaimed until March 1804; it took for granted a lay society in which the abolition of feudal servitudes had resulted in the existence of absolute property rights. Equality before the law, freedom of conscience and occupation, and the supremacy of the lay state were asserted. The ·careful regulations concerning inheritance, landed property, and mortgages, the provision that a testator could dispose freely of one-quarter of his estate, dividing the rest equally among his heirs, the recognition of divorce, and the large powers given to the head of a family—all contributed notably to the growth of an essentially bourgeois society. A Code of Civil Procedure, a Code of Criminal Procedure and Penal Law, a Rural Code, and a Commercial Code followed under the Empire. Strongly influenced by Roman law, these Codes left their indelible mark not only on France but on countries much farther afield. It must also be recorded that slavery, abolished in 1794, was restored in the colonies by a decree of May 1802.

Religious problems also cried out for solution, since the policies of the Civil Constitution of the Clergy had crumbled and the schism in the Gallican Church between "jurors" and "nonjurors" remained. The papacy under Pius VII, elected in 1800, showed itself receptive. After protracted negotiations both sides in July 1801 accepted the terms of a Concordat which was to last until 1905. Roman Catholicism was declared the religion of the majority of the French people, "and especially of the three consuls." Its faith was to be freely exercised in France, subject (significantly) to police regulations. Clergy were to accept the Republic by oath; Church lands were to remain in the hands of their new possessors; and all clerical salaries were to be paid by the state. Bishops, nominated by the first consul, were to be consecrated by the pope. They in turn nominated the parish clergy. These generally acceptable provisions were modified in 1802 by the Organic Articles, a series of police regulations issued without any consultation with Rome and deeply resented there. No papal bulls or decrees of Church councils would have effect without government approval, no papal legates could exercise authority in France, and the state declared its right to supervise Catholic schools and seminaries. In this way the old Gallican liberties were reasserted.[3] The Organic

---

[3] Thirty-eight nonjuring bishops refused to accept the Concordat, and some of them continued to administer small congregations making up what was known as the *Petite Eglise*. It still survives in a small western corner of France.

Articles also dealt with the Protestants, who were likewise subject to government regulation and were granted funds for the maintenance of their faith. In sum, though great difficulties with Rome were later to develop, a generally acceptable degree of religious order had been restored.

Other important steps were taken in the field of education, for despite a number of impressive documents issued during the revolutionary years little of substance had actually been achieved, save in the important field of technical training. A decree of March 1802 declared elementary schools to be the responsibility of the communes, while in each department secondary education would be provided by the *lycées*—boarding schools for boys entering at the age of twelve, with semimilitary discipline, uniforms, and training.

The Legion of Honor was created in 1802 to restore some of the symbols and dignities abolished a decade earlier. "Men," Napoleon told Thibaudeau, "are governed by baubles." The Legion of Honor was a reflection of the old orders of chivalry, with graded ranks, medals, ribbons, titles, and pensions. The insignia were modeled on those of the historic Order of St. Louis, and at the head was a grand chancellor whose palace to this day almost equals the presidential Elysée Palace in splendor. The importance of ceremonial was evident in other ways. Bonaparte and Josephine had first taken up their residence at the Luxembourg, soon moving to the Tuileries which was quickly refurbished and which, even under the Consulate, took on a ceremonial routine and etiquette reminiscent of the days of royalty. In Paris a style of building which added Egyptian, Etruscan, and Pompeiian elements to the massive Roman architectural tradition produced in time the Church of the Madeleine, the Bourse, the Vendôme Column, and the two triumphal arches—the Carrousel and the Arc de Triomphe. "*Ce qui est grand*," declared Napoleon, "*est toujours beau*"—"What is big is always beautiful."

The concentration of power continued. The Constitution of the Year VIII had provided Bonaparte with a ten-year term of office. Although several royalist attempts against his life were discovered, he felt a growing confidence in his position. Hence he had little difficulty in securing an overwhelmingly affirmative vote in a plebiscite of 1802 on the question of granting the three consuls life tenure. A decree of the Senate soon afterwards empowered the first consul to nominate the other two and to name his own successor. Further changes, embodied in what was called the Constitution of the Year X (1802) gave Bonaparte exclusive authority to choose the Senate, which was given the power to revise the constitution and to dissolve the two legislative bodies. The Tribunate, never a success, was reduced from one hundred to fifty members.

Under such conditions, and given both the character of Bonaparte and his irreparable breach with the Bourbons, personal, hereditary rule could not be far off. An episode played into his hands. A royalist plot early in 1804 seemed to implicate a young member of the great Condé family, the *émigré* duke of Enghien. In an outrageous disregard of law, Bonaparte sent a squadron of French hussars across the Rhine to seize the duke on the territory of Baden and escort him posthaste to Paris. At one o'clock in the morning he was brought before a hastily convened commission in the fortress of Vincennes where he was quickly found guilty and, within an hour and a half, shot. The grave outside the fortress had been dug before he arrived. Although the news shocked Europe, and provoked Talleyrand's famous remark, "It was worse than a crime; it was a blunder," the event still further discredited royalist conspirators and seems to have confirmed Bonaparte's overpowering confidence in his own destinies. At St. Helena he insisted that in like circumstances he would have acted again as he did then. A month later, in May 1804, the Tribunate having voted for the principle of hereditary rule, the Senate promulgated a decree creating an emperorship in the lineage and heredity of Napoleon Bonaparte. His power was unquestionably autocratic, yet by keeping the externals of the Constitution of 1799—universal suffrage, Council of State, Senate, Tribunate and Legislative Body—some sense of the republican tradition was preserved. More important, although a new Caesarism had been imposed upon France, the basic economic, social, and religious reforms of the Revolution were still in effect.

Napoleon was crowned emperor in a splendid ceremony at Notre Dame on an icy day in December 1804. Pius VII had been brusquely summoned to make the arduous trip across the Alps in order to be present and to bless, although not to crown, the emperor, who himself placed the crown upon his and Josephine's head. A new stage of the Napoleonic epic had begun.

Among the numerous striking achievements of this consular period one in conclusion deserves emphasis. Autocratic in temperament, Napoleon well knew the necessity of a trained and efficient bureaucracy. The Council of State which in its new form he created and dominated contained men—Talleyrand, Gaudin, and Roederer, for example—of high technical abilities. A striking innovation of 1803 was to attach *auditeurs* ("young men of promise,") to the Council so that they could be trained to become higher civil servants. By 1811 the *auditeurs* numbered over three hundred, and it has well been observed that in promoting their work Napoleon was fifty years ahead of his time. The Council of State, which today still sits in the Palais Royal, was in time to create an elaborate system of administrative law with the aid of which it supervised local administration and all public establishments. The Council has been described as the unshakable cornerstone of the French bureaucracy. "Napoleon's peculiar and lasting achievement," the late Professor Cobban has well written, "was the work of the Consulate—that administrative reorganization which, in perspective, can be seen as bequeathing not only to France but to much of the rest of the world the most powerful instrument of bureaucratic control that the Western world had known since the Roman Empire." [4]

Imperial France

The proclamation of the Empire in 1804 inevitably brought a new climate of grandeur to France. From then until 1815 the country remained almost constantly at war. Although an intoxicating series of victories demonstrated the power lying in the hands of the new Charlemagne, the price paid, nevertheless, was heavy, and in time a kind of war weariness settled upon France. After the Russian disaster of 1812 many Frenchmen were ready to accept a less spectacular and a less demanding regime.

Since Napoleon had proclaimed an hereditary empire, princely titles and estates were given to the members of his family. Changes in the political map of Europe eventually made Joseph king of Naples and then of Spain; Jerome became king of Westphalia; Louis became king of Holland; and Murat (a brother-in-law) followed Joseph as king of Naples. The chief French palaces—the Tuileries, the Grand Trianon, Saint-Cloud, Compiègne, and Fontainebleau—were expensively refurbished, and the smaller chateau of Malmaison was elegantly restored by Empress Josephine. An elaborate court ceremonial, much of it dictated explicitly by Napoleon, was put into effect. The public could enjoy military reviews, splendid *Te Deums*, and wide-ranging imperial tours of inspection. An elaborate new Napoleonic nobility was set up. Next in rank to the imperial family were the six grand imperial dignitaries, and following them the grand officers of the Empire. The title of marshal, given altogether to twenty-six of Napoleon's generals, was usually accompanied by the title of prince or duke, with appropriate landed endowments. Titles were bestowed in a graduated order—prince, duke, count, baron, and knight—corresponding to the public office held. Talleyrand, for example, as foreign minister became prince of Benevento; Fouché as minister of police was duke of Otranto; Corvisart, Napoleon's doctor, was a baron. It has been calculated that Napoleon created 10 princes, 31 dukes, 388

[4] A. Cobban, *A History of Modern France, II* (1965), 39–40.

counts, 1,090 barons, and 1,500 chevaliers. In addition many noblemen of
the old regime were induced to come back into the imperial service.
Not uncommonly they scoffed at the barrack-room manners, the arro-
gance, and the frequently vulgar display of the new elite. The wife of
Marshal Lefebvre, duke of Danzig, was a former washerwoman who not
withstanding this showed a total lack of embarrassment at her humble
origins. In the end some kind of accommodation was reached.

The divorce of Empress Josephine in 1809 was quickly followed by
Napoleon's marriage to the eighteen-year-old Marie-Louise, daughter of
Emperor Francis I of Austria. Josephine had borne Napoleon no children,
and an heir, so he felt, was imperative. A link with the Hapsburgs would
give further luster to the regime. After much diplomatic discussion and
inquiry the Austrian decision was made, and Marie-Louise, dispatched
posthaste to France, in 1811 bore Napoleon a son, given the title, king
of Rome.

The powerful bureaucratic machine which Napoleon had created
under the Consulate served him efficiently during the years of the Empire.
Some changes were made; the Tribunate, which had been weakened in
1803, was abolished in 1807 as being useless. Less attention was paid to the
Legislative Body; new laws often took the form simply of *consulta* ("decrees") issuing from the Senate. It was both a strength and a weakness
of this system that the driving force of Napoleon was apparent everywhere. His working day frequently lasted for eighteen hours. He could
preside for six hours at a stretch over a meeting of the Council of State,
where matters were often discussed in intricate detail. It is clear that in
these discussions differences of expert opinion were common. The emperor had a phenomenal memory for the endless reports, both military
and civil, that came regularly to him, and he could discover (and remem-
ber) a discrepancy of a few francs. On his campaigns dispatches from
Paris followed him everywhere, and he required secretaries always to be
in attendance. His published correspondence indicates that he dictated
an average of fifteen letters, many of them long and detailed, on every
day of his career. The superb abilities and driving energy of Napoleon
served him well—for a time. In the end he paid the price, for by 1809, at
the age of forty, he had become jealous, irritable, frequently unwell, and
unsure of his judgments. By 1812 he was at odds with nearly every member of his family. When he died at St. Helena, at the age of fifty-one, the
cause of his death appears to have been a cancerous, perforated gastric
ulcer.

Another authoritarian aspect of the imperial period lay in increasingly rigorous police and censorship methods. The ministry of police,
suppressed in 1802, was revived in 1804, and under Fouché became noto-

rious for its ruthless methods. In 1810 it was decreed that political suspects could be held without trial on the orders of the Council of State— a flagrant revival of the old *lettres de cachet*. A severe censorship, which confiscated the entire ten thousand copies of Madame de Staël's famous book *On Germany*, limited the number of Paris newspapers to four and allowed only one for each department. All were government controlled.

In the legal field further codes of law were prepared under the Empire: those of Civil Procedure and Criminal Procedure, the Penal Code, the Rural Code, and the Commercial Code. Trial by jury was curtailed and special courts were authorized to deal with cases of counterfeiting, smuggling, armed robbery, and rebellion. The Criminal Code even revived branding, and for parricide stipulated the cutting off of a hand followed by decapitation. Ruthless insistence upon order was in large respects taking the place of humane forms of justice.

An important question to ask is how far an empire so deeply involved in the strains of a great European war could maintain a thriving economy. The actual military drain upon French manpower seems to have been only moderate, for the nature of Napoleon's conquests made it possible for him to count heavily upon foreign levies of troops. The best calculations indicate that between 1800 and 1815 Napoleon called up about 2,000,000 men within the limits of the 1789 borders of France. Battle deaths and deaths from wounds have been estimated at 400,000. If these figures are compared with the 1,300,000 military deaths which a France of 40 million people endured in the much shorter period between 1914 and 1918, it will be seen that the bloodletting of the Napoleonic period could hardly have left any deep or permanent scar upon France.

Napoleon, with his passion for practical improvements, was always deeply concerned with the economic life of France. Here he could build upon the substantial foundations of the consular period, although throughout the imperial years his measures were inevitably affected by the pressures of war. Napoleon's fiscal policies benefited much from the able work of Gaudin as minister of finances. Though budgets turned out to be rarely in balance, between 430 million and 500 million francs were collected annually in taxes, and in 1813 the national debt had fallen to the astonishingly low figure of only 63 million francs. An attempt begun in 1807 to create a *cadastre*, or evaluation of all landed property, never succeeded in covering more than six thousand of the forty-four thousand communes in France. Indirect taxes were encouraged as being less visible, and therefore supposedly less painful; the chief of these were the revived salt tax of 1806 and excises on liquors, tobacco, and playing cards. The Bank of France was reorganized and enlarged in 1806 so as to make it more subject to the emperor, who selected its governors. In general

Napoleon despised the policy of seeking loans, though in 1815 he was forced to finance the Waterloo campaign through the speculator and financier Ouvrard, who had been imprisoned for several years, and who, as a deeply concerned creditor, was an eyewitness of the campaign.

Industrial life was encouraged, though never in such a way as to equal the burgeoning technological revolution in contemporary Britain. A tariff wall, chiefly directed against Britain, continued the policy first begun by the Convention in 1793. Some subsidies were given to industries, especially after the founding of the Ministry of Manufactures and Commerce in 1811. The famous loom designed most ingeniously by Joseph Jacquard to weave patterned silk fabrics led to substantial rewards and honors for its owner; by 1812 some eleven thousand of these Jacquard looms were in operation. Though cotton industry moved in the direction of mechanical spinning, with perhaps a million spindles ultimately in operation, the severe shortage of raw cotton caused plans for large increases in production to fail. The needs of war inevitably led to the widespread establishment of state factories for military purposes.

Agriculture, save in some areas, was quite generally prosperous. New crops were encouraged: sugar beets, chicory, cotton, mulberry bushes (for silk), tobacco, and the dyestuff, woad. In 1811, 80,000 acres of sugar beet were planted, the area rising in 1812 to 240,000 acres, with special refineries built to produce this beet sugar. Fairs were sponsored to encourage cattle and sheep breeding, and for the same purpose large numbers of merinos were brought in from Spain.

In many respects the French workers did not fare well. Though Napoleon sought strenuously to provide them with cheap food, he continued the practice of forbidding them to form associations, and in 1803 required all workers to carry a *livret*, or passbook, which, if not endorsed by their employer, made it impossible for them to take new jobs. This punitive system actually lasted until 1890. On the other hand the *conseils des prud'hommes*, or boards of responsible workers and employers first set up in 1806 to advise and rule on working conditions in certain towns and industries, were a notable step forward.

The encouragement of trade was an obvious necessity. New chambers of commerce were encouraged in addition to those begun under the *ancien régime*. A large industrial exposition was held at Paris in 1806. In fifteen years about forty thousand miles of road were built or improved, including carriage roads over the Simplon and Mont Cenis passes in the Alps. New canals linked the Rhine, the Rhône, the Somme, and the Scheldt; and the new service of bridges and highways constructed, among others, four bridges across the Seine in Paris and one over the Rhine at Kehl. Yet improvements in land transportation could not offset the enormous commercial advantage which England held on the seas, from which the French merchant marine had practically vanished. Foreign trade under the Empire was actually less than it had been in the closing days of the *ancien régime*.

Everything that Napoleon attempted to do in this commercial area was vitiated by those policies known as the Continental System.[5] Beginning with the Berlin Decrees of November 1806, Napoleon sought to keep goods from England and its colonies from entering the Continent, so that in essence the policy was one of boycott rather than embargo. Though England was hurt, especially in the years 1807 and 1808, the Continent suffered more, while by 1809 English exports reached a record height. Very inconsistently Napoleon was compelled at times to issue licenses authorizing the limited import of British colonial products, subject to high tariffs, into France. The years of depression between 1810 and 1812 did great harm, and in the end the disasters of war kept Napoleon from achieving the economic goals he had set for France.

In religious matters Napoleon continued the policy of control begun under the Consulate with respect to Catholics, Protestants, and Jews. The Catechism of the Empire, drawn up under Napoleon's directions in 1806, was to be used in all Catholic churches. It included the following:

> Christians owe to the princes who govern them, and we
> owe in particular to our Emperor Napoleon I, love, respect,
> obedience, fidelity, military service, and payments levied
> for the preservation and defense of the Empire and his
> throne.

Protestants and Jews continued to be recognized in their own organizations, the former being given separate arrangements for Calvinists and Lutherans, with salaries paid to their ministers. The government claimed the right to approve all doctrinal decisions and disciplinary changes. Napoleon authorized the Jews to work through a grand sanhedrin in order to distinguish between the unchanging features of Mosaic law and their changing political obligations. A decree of 1808 required all Jews publicly to declare a surname—a move intended, but with only partial success, to help in their assimilation.

Although the French public as a whole accepted the regime of the Concordat, great difficulties arose with Pope Pius VII, chiefly over the question of the Papal States. The Roman Republic set up in 1798 had lasted only a year, following which papal rule under French supervision

---

[5] This is discussed in more detail in the next chapter, pp. 114-115.

resumed. When the kingdom of Italy was created in 1805 from the former Italian Republic some outlying papal territories were added to it. Soon afterwards the ports of Ancona and Civita Vecchia were occupied. Finally, in 1808 a French army occupied Rome itself and in the following year the Papal States were annexed to France. Pius VII immediately excommunicated all "aggressors against the Holy See," though not mentioning Napoleon by name. In response to this Napoleonic officials, going beyond their orders, seized not only some papal officials but also Pius VII himself. He was held a virtual prisoner at Savona, near Genoa, until 1812 and then taken as an officially honored but certainly unwilling guest to Fontainebleau where his fine apartments can still be seen. In 1814 he returned to Rome—the victor in the end over Napoleon.

Concerned as he was with every aspect of French life, Napoleon gave much attention to education. Though the principles of free, compulsory state education had been established earlier, save in the field of technical training actual progress was not great. A number of *lycées* were added to those already started under the Consulate. Napoleon desired above all to have a unified system of teaching under the control of a strong, central hand. "The essential thing," he declared in 1805, "is a teaching body like that of the Jesuits of old." Deliberations in the Council of State resulted in the formal establishment of the Imperial University in 1808 —in reality resembling much more a ministry of education. Headed by a grand master, Fontanes, it was the culminating point of the teaching agencies in France, knitting them together into one system. "No one may open a school," the basic decree stated, "or teach publicly without being a member of the Imperial University and graduated from one of its faculties." Napoleon's position was explicitly stated: "We reserve to ourselves . . . to amend . . . every decision, regulation, or act emanating from the Council of the University or the Grand Master, whenever we shall deem it useful for the good of the State." Women's education was largely ignored. Napoleon's efforts could not keep many pupils from attending the already existing private secondary schools largely in the hands of the Church, and the struggle between the claims of an official system and those of the Church schools went on through the nineteenth and into the twentieth century.

Napoleon's policies were hardly favorable to the growth of the arts and literature, although he continued to embellish the great cities, above all Paris. Many ambitious projects remained on the drawing boards: plans for impressive markets and slaughterhouses, new gateways at the main entrances to the capital, new theaters, huge additions to the Louvre, a vast palace for the king of Rome where the Palais de Chaillot now stands, and an enormous stone elephant, water spouting from its upturned trunk, intended however incongruously to dominate the Place de la Bastille.[6] The age showed no great growth in imaginative literature. The poet André Chénier had been guillotined under the Terror. François de Chateaubriand completed his *Genius of Christianity* in 1802, a work which opened the door to the coming age of romanticism. He served for a time in diplomatic posts but resigned in protest against the execution of the duke of Enghien. In 1814 his pen was to denounce Bonaparte and welcome back the Bourbons. Similarly, Benjamin Constant, whom Napoleon had made a member of the Tribunate, soon left France. Madame de Staël, who had at first hailed (and indeed pursued) Bonaparte, quickly aroused his violent opposition. Her novels *Delphine* and *Corinne* were important in the transition from the classical to the romantic age, and her notable study *On Germany* was a landmark. She wrote very acutely and with a strong liberal bent on political subjects. Napoleon, who described her variously as "a veritable pest," "an old crow," and "a madwoman who should be taken into custody," confiscated her books and forbade her to reside in Paris. Abroad, she became a leading critic of the imperial despotism and was known perhaps not unfairly as "the conscience of Europe." In the prevalent atmosphere of repression, literature in France could hardly flourish.

[6] The sad history of the Elephant of the Bastille deserves a footnote. The emperor spent at least a million francs in having models made, building a granite foundation, and erecting thereupon a huge wood-and-plaster monument which stood in decaying grandeur, haunted by rats and overgrown with weeds until 1848, when the Republic had it destroyed. Victor Hugo, who lived nearby in the Place des Vosges, noted the extraordinary impression created in the moonlight by this melancholy legacy of a great age.

7

NAPOLEONIC EUROPE

The New Charlemagne

For at least a decade the history of Europe and the personal career of Napoleon were almost synonymous. The Peace of Amiens with Britain in 1802 soon proved to be only a truce, so that before the transition from Consulate to Empire had been effected France was again to be at war. It was to remain at war, with a few intermissions, until 1815.

That Napoleon's ambitions reached far beyond the frontiers of his country can be seen clearly in the colonial sphere. Despite France's colonial losses in the eighteenth century it still held a substantial empire which Napoleon wanted to enlarge. True, his Egyptian expedition had been a failure, and he was unable to hold the Ionian Islands promised to him at Campo Formio or to keep the English from seizing Malta. By contrast, the New World seemed to hold great promise. In 1795 France had acquired full possession of Santo Domingo and by the secret treaty of 1800 had secured Louisiana from Spain. On this island a talented Negro leader, Toussaint L'Ouverture, established what was in essence a Negro republic. Hence in 1802 Napoleon sent an army of 33,000 men commanded by his brother-in-law General Leclerc, ostensibly to be military governor but actually instructed to overthrow Toussaint. This he did, and Toussaint died in 1803 in a French prison. By a decree of May 1802 Napoleon reestablished slavery in the French colonies. The victory was hollow, for the yellow fever destroyed Leclerc and two-thirds of his men, while another Negro leader, Jean Jacques Dessalines, took over the island in 1804, assumed the title of emperor of Haiti, and ordered the massacre of the white population. In August 1803 the momentous decision was taken by Napoleon to abandon his American adventures and sell the vast Louisiana Territory to the United States.

Concurrently, Napoleon moved even farther afield. In 1800 an expedition was sent to Australia, where for three years it mapped and surveyed the coasts. The only tangible outcome was a chart published at Paris in 1807 showing half of the Australian continent under the name of "Terre Napoléon." India had been in the background of Napoleon's plans at the time of the Egyptian expedition, and even earlier the Directory had shown its sympathy for Tippoo, sultan of Mysore, who was in revolt against the English, making him an honorary French citizen. Napoleon infuriated the English when in January 1803 he caused a report by General Sebastiani, who had been sent on a secret mission to Egypt, to be published in the *Moniteur*. This declared that with an army of six thousand France could easily capture the country. Two months later a small French naval expedition was sent around the Cape of Good Hope to India, with instructions to reinforce the few French garrisons there and pointing out the possible "great glory" to be won. Though nothing came of this expedition, Napoleon's oriental dreams remained still alive. They were renewed from time to time over the years, most notably in the fantastic proposal made to Tsar Alexander I in 1808 for a joint Franco-Russian overland expedition of fifty thousand men to India.

While colonial projects turned out to be largely dreams, expansion in Europe quickly became a powerful reality. The settlements of 1801 and 1802 with Austria and Britain had been predicated on the fact of a general peace. Napoleon's European meddlings, however, were endless. The Treaty of Lunéville had authorized France to take the lead in finding lands within Germany for dispossessed Rhineland princes. The real work was undertaken by Talleyrand in Paris, on the general principle that the many still remaining ecclesiastical states as well as other very small German states would have to be destroyed. When the work was done (to the great financial advantage of Talleyrand), out of seventy-four ecclesiastical states only the archbishopric of Mainz remained. The free imperial cities were reduced from fifty-one to six. The principal beneficiaries, in addition to the dispossessed Rhineland princes, were the already substantial states of Prussia, Bavaria, Hanover, Württemberg, and Hesse-Cassel. In sum, about one-sixth of the population of the Holy Roman Empire—about four million people—was transferred from ecclesiastical to secular rule. This striking example of Napoleonic simplification

and reorganization within Germany was embodied in a decree of the
Imperial Diet, the famous *Reichsdeputationshauptschluss* of 1803.

Further European transformations went on. Tuscany was converted
in 1801 into the kingdom of Etruria, supposedly to be ruled by a Spanish
prince but soon to become French, and in the same year the Batavian Republic was forced to accept a new constitution in spite of the vigorous rejection of this in a Dutch plebiscite. The Cisalpine Republic was changed
in 1802 into the Italian Republic with Napoleon as president, while Piedmont, long in French hands, was formally annexed. Troubles in Switzerland led to a French invasion, the outcome being that Swiss commissioners
were summoned to Paris to accept the constitution drawn up for them by
Napoleon and to ally with France. This Act of Mediation (1802) gave
Switzerland a federal structure of nineteen cantons, essentially what it
has today.

In the light of all these circumstances Britain refused to return Malta
to the Knights of St. John as it had agreed to do in the Peace of Amiens.
Stormy negotiations dragged on in Paris, only to end with the renewal of
war in May 1803—a war that was to continue until Napoleon's downfall.
Russia, increasingly incensed at French policy and urged strongly by
Britain, broke off diplomatic relations in September 1804 and in the
following April formally allied itself with Britain. Napoleon meanwhile
continued with additional dramatic European changes. Early in 1805 the
Italian Republic became the kingdom of Italy and in May, in a spectacular
ceremony held in Milan Cathedral, Napoleon was crowned with the
historic iron crown of Lombardy. In the same year Genoa was annexed
to France, while the small Italian principalities of Piombino and Lucca
were made into "imperial fiefs" and given to Napoleon's sisters, Elisa and
Pauline. Not surprisingly Austria, deeply concerned at the seemingly
endless German and Italian changes, felt compelled to enter the war,
secretly joining the Anglo-Russian alliance in August 1805 and bringing
with it the kingdom of Naples. Prussia alone of the major powers refused
to enter the war.

The War of the Third Coalition saw Napoleon's military powers at
their very highest. His first plans to invade England unquestionably were
seriously intended, for an army of 170,000 men was assembled and trained
near Boulogne, special roads built, and over two thousand flat-bottomed
invasion barges assembled. He could not, however, win even temporary
control of the seas, and Nelson's victory at Trafalgar in October 1805—
one of the greatest in naval history—ended any danger of French challenge
on the high seas. Two months before Trafalgar Napoleon had realized the
situation, had begun to move troops from Boulogne, and had taken them

across Europe at top speed against the Austrians. His victory at Ulm in October was followed by the devastating defeat of a combined Austro-Russian army at Austerlitz in December. These were huge battles, with from 70,000 to 90,000 troops engaged on either side and with the kind of bloody casualties that such hand-to-hand encounter inflicts.

For the third time in eight years Austria was compelled to seek peace. The Treaty of Pressburg (December 1805) required Austria to relinquish Venetia, Istria, and Dalmatia, also yielding the Tyrol to Bavaria and some smaller possessions to Württemberg and Baden. The leniency of the earlier treaties had vanished and it was clear that the days of the Holy Roman Empire were numbered, for Austria was now completely excluded from Italy and southern Germany.

Prussia's turn came next. In December on the promise of Hanover it had allied with France. Following the death of William Pitt, England in the ensuing summer undertook secret negotiations with France during which France indicated that England might be given Hanover. Even though England refused this offer Prussia was infuriated, and still more so at the repressive measures taken by Napoleon in Germany. In September, consequently, Prussia recklessly reversed its policy and declared war upon France. Seldom has a major power acted more rashly. Within a month the Prussian armies were overwhelmed at Jena, French troops paraded victoriously along *Unter den Linden* in Berlin, and Frederick William III had to flee ignominiously to the easternmost tip of his lands at Memel. Only Russia could now maintain the European land conflict, and it, too, after the indecisive winter battle of Eylau met defeat at Friedland in June 1807. What is known as the Fourth Coalition was now at an end.

In the year preceding the Treaty of Tilsit, dictated in July 1807 to Prussia and Russia, Napoleon had dramatically demonstrated his power. His brother Joseph was made king of Naples and his brother Louis, king of Holland. In July 1806 a plan prepared in Paris had combined sixteen states of western Germany into the Confederation of the Rhine. One of these states, the Grand Duchy of Berg, was allotted to Napoleon's brother-in-law Murat. In 1807 another new state composed in large part of forfeited Prussian lands, the kingdom of Westphalia, was given to Napoleon's brother Jerome.[1]

The 1807 Treaty of Tilsit dictated to Prussia on the banks of the River Niemen was savage. Prussia lost every inch of its land west of the River Elbe, thus being excluded from the Confederation of the Rhine, the existence of which it now had to recognize. It also had to give up its

[1] To assume this crown Jerome was required to abandon his American wife, the former Miss Patterson of Baltimore, and marry a German princess.

Polish provinces to another new creation, the Grand Duchy of Warsaw—
the eastern counterpart of the Confederation of the Rhine. French troops
were to garrison all Prussian fortified towns until an indemnity of un-
specified amount was paid. Prussia was to close its ports to English shipping and promised to join France against England if an honorable peace
had not been reached by December. A year later the size of the Prussian
army was limited to forty-three thousand men.

The terms given to Russia were by contrast surprisingly lenient, for
Napoleon as an emperor had hailed Tsar Alexander as a brother. Russia
recognized the changes being made in Europe, gave up the Ionian Islands,
closed its ports to British shipping, and agreed to an eventual war with
Britain if it refused Alexander's mediation. In somewhat ambiguous
terms a secret article implied that Russia might someday share in a partition of the European parts of the Ottoman Empire.

To crown his triumphs Napoleon informed the Imperial Diet in
August 1806 that he no longer recognized the existence of the Holy
Roman Empire, its former head now becoming Francis I, hereditary
emperor of Austria. By his various German policies Napoleon had created,
though only to last for a short time, what has been called "the German
Triad," the three parts of which were the Confederation of the Rhine, a
much weakened Austria, and a much weakened Prussia. Far more effectively than had been the case with Richelieu and Mazarin he sought to
make the threefold division of Germany a means to ensure the preponderance of France.

Since England was still undefeated, some new means must be sought
to win victory. The Continental System was Napoleon's plan for this end.
He had set up a high tariff against England in 1803, and had tried later
to close the North Sea ports to English goods. The Berlin Decree of
November 1806 declared the British Isles to be in a state of blockade,
although France obviously did not possess the naval forces that such a
blockade would require. In essence the program was really one of boycott. All goods on the Continent belonging to or coming from Great
Britain and its colonies were to be seized. The British answer came in the
Orders in Council of November 1806 and January 1807 which declared
that all neutral ships obeying the Berlin Decrees would be liable to capture, and that any neutral ship must obtain a license at an English port
and pay a heavy duty before proceeding to the Continent. By further
decrees issued at Fontainebleau and Milan Napoleon announced that
neutrals obeying the Orders in Council would be treated as if they were
British. It is clear that both sides were making havoc of neutral rights,
one outcome being that the United States and Britain in 1812 were for a
time briefly at war.

In summary, Napoleon's Continental System did not work. England, after experiencing the two hard years of 1807 and 1808 and again in 1811, was to enlarge its export trade, thanks in part to new markets opening in South America. The system caused great hardship on the Continent, it created much unrest, and it led Napoleon to ever wider policies of intervention, most notably in Spain. The kingdom of Etruria (Tuscany) was annexed to France in 1808, the Papal States in 1809, Holland in 1810, and the German coastline as far as the Elbe in the same year. Each side took steps inconsistent with a true policy of blockade: England forced colonial wares into Europe by means of bribery, smuggling, and the use of new routes as far afield as the Balkans, while the French at times issued special licenses, regularized in the Trianon Decree of 1810, to admit colonial products on payment of a 50 percent duty. In this way Napoleon hoped that both goods and revenues would be secured. In hard fact the confusions of the Continental System make it clear that, rather than serve Napoleon's purposes, it contributed substantially to his eventual downfall.

The first great warning signal to France came in Spain, a country which, allied with Napoleon, had shared in the French defeat at Trafalgar. It had at first accepted the demands of the Continental System and had agreed in October 1807 to join in the partition of Portugal, permitting French troops to pass through Spain and seize Lisbon. A palace revolution of March 1808 enabled the incompetent heir-apparent, Ferdinand, to overthrow his equally incompetent father, Charles IV, and claim the throne. Napoleon summoned the precious pair to Bayonne, presumably to negotiate. Instead, they were unceremoniously held in France and Napoleon's brother Joseph was quickly transferred from Naples to Madrid to be Spain's new ruler. The Spanish at once rose in protest, forcing a small French army sent against them to capitulate. The British in August 1808 landed a small force in Portugal, counting on the support of large numbers of Spanish and Portuguese regulars and guerillas. It was evident that the local committees (*Juntas*) directing the fighting were moving in the direction of a larger organization, for when a Spanish parliament, the *Cortes*, was convoked at Cadiz in 1810 something resembling a national opposition in Spain to Napoleon had finally appeared.

Although the first British expedition to Portugal withdrew in the spring of 1809, a larger force soon returned under the command of the duke of Wellington and established itself near Lisbon behind the famous lines of Torres Vedras—the first great modern employment of the techniques of trench warfare. In the spring of 1811 Wellington was able to break out of his lines and by the end of the year to clear Portugal of French troops. To meet the mounting crisis in Spain Napoleon was obliged to send some of his best generals, to go there for a time himself,

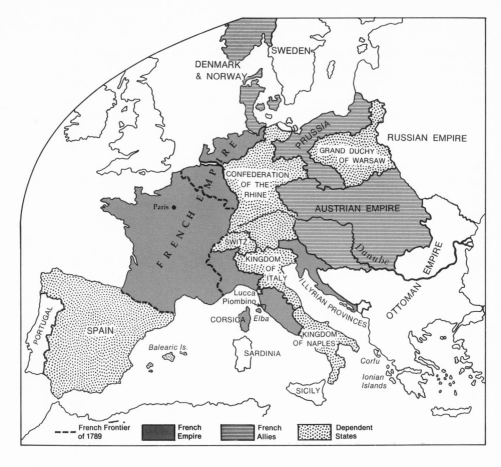

NAPOLEONIC EUROPE IN 1810

Despite the enormous areas brought under control by Napoleon, the frontiers established for France in November 1815 were essentially the Bourbon frontiers of 1789.

and by 1810 to commit the enormous total of 370,000 troops. Yet all attempts to control what Napoleon called "the Spanish ulcer" failed; Wellington's steady advance led to the fall of Madrid in August 1812, and by the summer of 1813 he was at the Pyrenees. Like the Continental System, the Peninsular War raised an ominous threat to the continuance of Napoleonic Europe.

One further military development occurred in these heady years of Napoleonic domination. Most surprisingly a thrice-defeated Austria in 1809 took up the sword again. The reasons were complex. A new group of young leaders bitterly resented the 1805 Peace of Pressburg. Peasants in the Tyrol, an area transferred in 1805 to Bavaria, loyally sought to rejoin Austria. War spirit in Vienna was deliberately whipped up in a press and pamphlet campaign which was one of the first examples of its kind. England exerted strong diplomatic pressure and promised large subsidies. Believing that Napoleon was deeply involved in Spain, Austria in March 1809 declared war on France. The response was immediate. By May Napoleon had assembled 200,000 men in Germany and had occupied Vienna. Although the Battle of Aspern was in reality a defeat for the French, who suffered 20,000 casualties, Napoleon's July victory at Wagram—the greatest artillery battle yet known—redressed the situation. A British attempt to create a diversion by landing troops on the Dutch coast was a disastrous failure so that by October Austria was ready to sign the Peace of Schönbruun. By its terms Austria lost Austrian Galicia to the Grand Duchy of Warsaw, Salzburg to Bavaria, and the Adriatic areas of Trieste, Carinthia, and Carniola directly to France. These last surrenders made Austria a completely landlocked power, now burdened with a heavy indemnity, forced to accept the Continental System, allied to France, and counting itself three and a half million subjects the poorer.

The Downfall

By 1810, when the Empire had reached its greatest extent(See map, p. 116.), the mounting list of Napoleon's mistakes and failures had become striking. His brutal treatment of Pope Pius VII and the annexation to France of all papal territories suggested a will that would brook no opposition. Talleyrand, Napoleon's ablest minister, resigned from the foreign office in 1807, and Fouché was dismissed from the ministry of police in 1810. Their successors were both nonentities, and while Talleyrand retained his position in the Council of State both he and Fouché secretly began to work against the emperor. Marshal Bernadotte, whose conduct had always been devious, in 1810 was invited by the Swedes to become their crown prince and virtual ruler, since the elderly Charles XIII had become senile. Bernadotte soon was to set his own ambitions against those of Napoleon. In the face of British seapower the Continental System did little more than create an even larger continental discontent. The Spanish imbroglio grew steadily worse. The stern treatment meted out to Prussia at Tilsit in 1807 and to Austria in 1805 and 1809 led to the beginnings of a nationalist resentment that soon spread beyond Austria and Prussia into other parts of Germany. Within Prussia a remarkable group of civil servants—Stein, Hardenberg, Gneisenau, Scharnhorst, and Humboldt—began to transform the state. Even more basically important, a number of distinguished literary figures, building upon the foundations laid in Herder's writings, were evoking a new concept of the German Fatherland.

The immediate critical problems arose with Russia, where Alexander I, an enigmatic figure touched by a strong element of religious mysticism, soon departed from the outward friendship which both emperors had displayed at Tilsit. He resented Napoleon's enlargement of the Grand Duchy of Warsaw in 1809. He was a reluctant partner in the Continental System, which worked strongly to Russia's disadvantage. He had been repeatedly put off in his hopes for a partition of the Ottoman Empire. He had been offended when Napoleon, after inquiring about the suitability of Alexander's sister as a bride, turned instead to an Austrian choice. During the glittering 1808 meeting of the two emperors at Erfurt, Talleyrand had hinted to Alexander that the Napoleonic regime could not last. Still another irritant was Napoleon's annexation in 1810 of Oldenburg, a German grand duchy whose heir-apparent was married to Alexander's sister. Above all, the tsar had developed an extraordinary sense of his regenerative mission as the leader of Europe, a mission to which in every respect Napoleon, the heir of the Revolution, seemed opposed.

By 1811 a breach between Russia and France was imminent. Napoleon then undertook his military preparations, beginning to assemble from all the parts of Europe subject to his authority a vast army of 600,000 men of which only a minority (about 200,000) were actually French. Without bothering to declare war or even to announce his actions to the French people, Napoleon crossed the River Niemen in June 1812 with 450,000 men, planning characteristically to separate the Russian armies and destroy them one by one. Of necessity, rather than by any well-planned grand strategy, the Russians adopted a policy of retreat—in the modern phrase trading space for time, refusing fixed battles, and constantly harassing the French advance. At Borodino in September Napoleon did fight what he later called "the most terrible of all my battles"—a bloody conflict which in one day cost the Russians 50,000 casualties and the

French 30,000. A week after the battle Napoleon was in Moscow. Yet the main Russian armies were still intact, and on the very day of the French arrival the great city, still largely built of wood, began to go up in flames. The conflagration, so the evidence now shows, was undoubtedly the deliberate act of the Russian governor. Short of supplies and without housing, Napoleon had no choice but to adopt the strategy of retreat.

The last, disastrous half of the campaign began in mid-October and with only 100,000 troops remaining under Napoleon's command. Although he later claimed that unexpectedly harsh weather caused the ensuing catastrophe, meteorological evidence shows that October was in fact unusually mild, and that the first snows did not come until November 5, when two-thirds of the return march had been completed. Desertions, illness, starvation, and constant Cossack harassment resulted in Napoleon's crossing the icy Beresina River late in November with only 40,000 men left. When the Grand Army reached the Niemen, the point of the original June departure, the survivors, along with reassembled garrison troops and other miscellaneous forces, totalled perhaps 100,000—all that remained of an original 600,000 men. Most ominously, the majority of the superb regiments of the Imperial Guard, which in 1810 had been brought up to a strength of 80,000 and of which 50,000 had marched, had been lost in the Russian snows. Marshal Berthier reported on December 12 to Napoleon, who had already left secretly for Paris, that less than five hundred of the Imperial Guard still remained under his command.

The years 1813 and 1814 were a veritable Twilight of the Gods—a collapse of the Napoleonic Empire in relation to which Napoleon's return from Elba in 1815 and the events of the ensuing Hundred Days were to prove only a disastrous epilogue. The beginning of the end came with the Russian decision, strongly pushed by Tsar Alexander, to follow the French armies across the Russian frontier and seek a decisive military victory in the west. Bernadotte, on the promise of support in gaining Norway and perhaps even the throne of France, had allied Sweden with Russia in 1812. Prussia followed, making a secret treaty with Russia early in 1813. Against these dangers Napoleon managed by an early call-up of the levies for 1813 and 1814 to put 250,000 men once more in the field, many of them poorly trained. After some indecisive battles in Saxony, however, he agreed in June to a two months' armistice. In the course of the negotiations, which included a dramatic nine-hour private interview at Dresden with Metternich, Napoleon made it clear to the Austrian foreign minister that he would not surrender the Grand Empire. "My domination," he told Metternich, "will not survive the day when I cease to be strong, and therefore feared."

The decisive turning point came when the armistice expired in mid-August and Austria made the crucial decision to join the Fifth Coalition. Napoleon, who had by that time brought his total forces in Germany up to 470,000 men, planned a campaign on a gigantic scale. He won a great battle near Dresden, but he was unable to stem the enormous tide of Russian, Prussian, Austrian, and Swedish troops converging against him. At Leipzig, in October, the fateful Battle of the Nations was fought in which the French with 160,000 troops and the Allies with more than 300,000 each lost some 60,000 men. It was a disaster for Napoleon who now had no choice but to retreat directly to the French frontier, witnessing the Confederation of the Rhine crumble around him as he marched.

At this point the Allies were determined upon the defeat of Napoleon but not necessarily upon the overthrow of his dynasty. A possible solution, for example, might have been a regency under Marie-Louise on behalf of Napoleon's infant son, the king of Rome. When the heads of the coalition approached the Rhine in November, they put forward the "Frankfurt Offer." This was conveyed to Napoleon as meaning that he could remain in power if he would withdraw to the "natural frontiers"—the Rhine, the Alps, and the Pyrenees. The actual public proclamation from Frankfurt was evasive, offering him only "an extent of territory unknown to France under its kings." Mistrusting even these offers, Napoleon undertook in the opening months of 1814 the celebrated "Campaign of France," retreating steadily from the Rhine and across the plains of Champagne towards Paris. His tactical brilliance has been compared to that of the Italian campaign of 1796, but although he won battle after battle the enormous weight of the Allied advance forced him steadily back towards Paris. In February and March new proposals were submitted to Napoleon by the Allies which would have substituted the Bourbon frontiers of 1792 for the "natural limits"—a loss of every inch of revolutionary conquest. These terms Napoleon again refused. The Allies consequently signed in March the Treaty of Chaumont, agreeing to remain united for twenty years against any possible future French aggression and stipulating in secret articles that France must return to the frontiers of 1792. Even at this date no agreement was reached as to a Bourbon restoration. In the view of Lord Castlereagh, the British foreign minister, this restoration, although he favored it, was a decision to be made by the French themselves.

Intrigues in Paris led by Talleyrand favored the Bourbon cause, as did the advance of the duke of Wellington across the Pyrenees into France. When he reached Bordeaux he found the white cockade of the Bourbons publicly displayed amid cries of "Vive le Roi!" Royalism, indeed, was emerging aboveground in wide areas, though in modest numbers. Napoleon had unwisely put Joseph Bonaparte in command of Paris and ordered him to defend it to the last. On the night of March 30, when the bonfires of the allied armies shone over the city from the heights of Montmartre, Joseph surrendered the capital without a shot fired, and on the following day the monarchs of Russia and Prussia made their triumphant entry. Huge masses of Russian, Austrian, and Prussian troops bivouacked along the Champs Elysées and in the Bois de Boulogne.[2] The Senate voted the deposition of Napoleon on April 3 and three days later voted the recall of Louis XVIII. His brother, the count of Artois, made a solemn entry into the capital on April 12, and on May 3 the king's procession entered Paris. Talleyrand, the servant of all regimes and henceforth claiming to be the principal architect of the Bourbon restoration, had already formed a provisional government. In his *Memoirs* he later made the famous statement, "I have never conspired save when I had the majority of Frenchmen for my accomplices."

Napoleon, deserted by his marshals and by his family, accepted on April 11 the Treaty of Fontainebleau, abdicating unconditionally. All members of his family were promised substantial settlements, and he was given the tiny island of Elba, off the Tuscan coast, where he would rule in full sovereignty.

The immediate future of France was settled by the First Treaty of Paris (May 1814), negotiated by Talleyrand with the victorious powers. It was surprisingly lenient. France went back to the old frontiers of 1792 and in addition received certain areas (part of Savoy and some fortified border towns in the northeast) intended to ensure a defensible frontier. France yielded Mauritius in the Indian Ocean and Tobago and St. Lucia in the West Indies to Britain, and also recognized Britain's possession of Malta. It even kept the art treasures seized by Napoleon and was not required to pay any indemnity or maintain an army of occupation. Such terms were a model of leniency, reflecting the Allied willingness to deal generously with the restored Bourbon monarchy. The treaty further announced that within two months a great general congress would meet at Vienna to dispose of the vast European areas so completely transformed by Napoleon; secret articles outlined plans for the general disposition of some of these areas. The essential purpose was to create buffer zones along the French borders which, in direct contrast to the sister republics policy of the Directory, were intended to make impossible any future French aggression.

Napoleon's return from Elba in March 1815, followed by the dra-

---

[2] Russian troops cut down so many trees for firewood in the Bois de Boulogne that the whole park subsequently had to be replanted.

matic events of the Hundred Days served little ultimate purpose save to display once more the tireless nature of his ambitions. His advance from the Mediterranean coast to Paris turned into a triumph. Twenty-four hours before he entered the Tuileries the unglamorous Louis XVIII fled his palace for the safety of Brussels. The Congress of Vienna declared that Napoleon had lost the only legal title remaining to him and that he was to be considered an object of public vengence. At Paris Napoleon invited Benjamin Constant to help in drafting the "Additional Act to the Constitutions of the Empire," proclaimed on June 1 and promising France supposedly liberal institutions with guarantees of civil liberties, a responsible ministry, an hereditary upper house, and a lower house based on some semblance of popular election. The time was in fact far too late for such proposals, for in harsh reality the only decisions that now mattered were military. Once again Napoleon put together an army totalling some 200,000 troops, of which no more than 130,000 were available as a striking force. The massive armies of the Allies—not, to be sure, all concentrated—numbered at least 800,000. In the Battle of Waterloo, fought in Belgium on June 18, Napoleon did have an immediate superiority of numbers, but even if he had not lost this "decisive" battle to Wellington his fate could hardly have been other than what it was. A shattered Napoleon signed a second abdication, then surrendered to the British, asking to be allowed to live in seclusion in a Scottish castle. Instead, he was sent on a British warship to the remote South Atlantic island of St. Helena where in May 1821, at the age of fifty-one and after six years of bitter and humiliating exile, he died.

The Napoleonic epic properly closed with the Second Treaty of Paris, agreed to in November 1815, when the rallying of the French to Napoleon had made the generous terms of the earlier 1814 treaty no longer acceptable. By this time the Bourbons were back once again, and it was they who had to accept terms which still gave France substantially the frontiers of 1792, but with the loss of those small additions conceded to it in 1814. France, moreover, now had to pay an indemnity of 700 million francs (a truly modest sum) and to support a small army of occupation. Although it was provided that the most important art works seized by Napoleon should be returned, and many in fact were (including the Venus de Medicis taken from Florence and the bronze horses taken from Venice), others, hidden in the cellars of the Louvre, escaped the inexpert eyes of the Allied commissioners.

The Legacy

So grand and sweeping a history as that of Napoleon defies any simple summary. Within France he had preserved the essential gains of the Revolution—the end of the feudal regime, the large-scale transfer of landed property from the Church and aristocratic hands to bourgeois and peasant owners, the abolition of noble and ecclesiastical privileges, the new legal system, and, if not liberty for all men, that kind of equality implicit in the phrases, "the career open to talent" and "a field-marshal's baton in every soldier's knapsack." Above all, Napoleon had taken the administrative and financial institutions created under the Revolution, both local and national, and welded them into a massive structure the weight of which is still everywhere discernible in France. His reforms had been chiefly the work of the consular period, a work so basic and substantial as to permit many good republican Frenchmen today still to describe themselves as "Bonapartistes du Consulat."

The year 1805 stands as the fateful turning point. Unhappily, as the regime became more authoritarian, as the police power grew, as war succeeded war, and as Napoleon's own ruthless disregard for human values became more apparent, the picture was clouded, and the price paid by France for the great Napoleonic reforms and for a few years of unparalleled splendor becomes hard to assess. In the end, it is true, the majority of Frenchmen turned with some relief to a less dominating and less demanding regime.

What had Napoleon accomplished in Europe? Never before, and perhaps never since, had the map of Europe been changed so extensively and so quickly as it was in the Napoleonic years. (See map, p. 116.) Napoleonic Europe at its greatest extent meant, first, a vastly enlarged France, reaching as far even as the Illyrian Provinces and absorbing within it the Kingdom of Holland—itself a Napoleonic creation. Substantial parts of Italy were included. This was "the Empire of the French." Beyond this lay lands making up "the Grand Empire," composed of states under Napoleon's control and in many cases ruled by members of his family. These were Spain (though only for a short time and very shakily), the Confederation of the Rhine (including the kingdom of Westphalia), Switzerland, the kingdom of Italy, the kingdom of Naples, the principalities of Lucca and Piombino, and the Grand Duchy of Warsaw. In a third category were states allied to France and in some measure under its influence: Prussia and Austria for a time, and the joint kingdom of Denmark and Norway. True, the Congress of Vienna in 1814 and 1815 set its purpose to be that of restoring Europe's legitimate rulers, and to a considerable extent it succeeded. Yet not all was restored, and the succeeding age of nation states has its roots in the changes beginning to appear during the revolutionary and Napoleonic periods.

Both in Italy and Germany the durable effects were felt. In western Germany the old ecclesiastical states and the meaningless petty principalities could never be restored. In Italy, though the state system of 1815 roughly resembled that of 1789, a suggestion of the need for unification still remained, to burst into splendid flower during the Risorgimento. The Grand Duchy of Warsaw, too, was one step along the road leading to the ultimate emergence of an independent Poland after its total disappearance in the partitions of the eighteenth century.

Was the foreign policy of the Empire simply one of aggression and conquest? Some distinguished French historians have maintained that to the contrary Napoleon's essential purpose was to preserve the justifiable gains won earlier during the years of the Convention and the Directory—the "natural frontiers" of France—and that to do this he had to campaign ever farther afield against monarchs who represented an older, discredited order. To accept this thesis strains human credence. By 1810 Amsterdam, Hamburg, and even Lübeck on the Baltic, as well as Genoa, Turin, Florence, and Rome in Italy were included within the limits of "France" with little more than the status of departmental capitals. By 1812 the 83 departments recognized in the Constitution of 1791 had risen to a total of 131. The population of this larger France was estimated then to have reached 42.7 millions of which something short of 27 millions lay within the prerevolutionary boundaries.

It has also been said of Napoleon that beyond his policies of military conquest and annexation he had dreams, far in advance of his time, of a united Europe. Las Cases reports him as speaking at St. Helena in 1816 in the following terms:

> . . . There are in Europe—though scattered—more than
> thirty million Frenchmen, fifteen million Spaniards, fifteen
> million Italians, thirty million Germans. I should have liked
> to make out of each of these people one single and uniform
> national body. . . . Then, perhaps, with the help of the
> univeral spread of education, it would have been possible to
> dream of applying the American constitution to the great
> European family.[3]

If these were dreams, there were also others, such as making a splendidly embellished Paris the capital of this new Europe and even of assembling there not only art treasures but also documents from the Vatican archives,

[3] C. Herold, *The Mind of Napoleon* (1965), p. 243.

from the great Spanish collections at Simancas, and from the archives of the Holy Roman Empire. As dreams they vanished, leaving the realities very different.

The balance between the good and the harm done by Napoleon in Europe is hard to establish. His brothers on the thrones of Holland, Naples, Westphalia, and Spain were in general a vulgar, unimpressive, and selfish crew. Historians, it is true, have made some attempt to establish the well-intentioned Joseph as an enlightened ruler of Naples, yet, though enlightened he may have been, desire outran performance. What the new rulers could not themselves do was in some degree achieved by Napoleonic administrators. The reforms upon which Napoleon insisted meant roads, schools, public works, in some areas the abolition of serfdom, improved justice, an attack on the "dead hand" of the Church, and an orderly system of finances. During the campaign of 1812 Napoleon actually drafted an edict for the emancipation of the Russian serfs, but whatever its purposes it had no chance of being put into effect. In contrast, conscription, monetary tribute, and the ever-present secret police made up the dark side of the picture. The reforms, moreover, were clearly intended more to serve the purposes of imperial France than to improve the lot of the subject peoples.

A striking outcome of the Napoleonic period was what has been called "the awakening of Europe"—the ultimate rising of one country after another, sometimes under new leaders, to oppose French domination. Elements of this awakening were discernible in Spain, Italy, and even more in Germany, where a truly national revival began to develop. Even in Russia some germs of a national sentiment are to be found. The Soviet historian Eugene Tarle, referring in this connection to one of his country's most famous patriotic poets, has written, "Without 1812 there would have been no Pushkin." Yet it has also been observed that conscript and professional armies serving the cause of the old monarchies, rather than any new national and citizen forces, were responsible for the final defeat of Napoleon.

In short, any estimate of Napoleon's place in history encounters the baffling problem of what happens when an individual of unusual, perhaps even unique, genius attempts to master the vast complexities of human affairs. A final, precise evaluation is impossible. The outward result for Napoleon was failure. "What a romance," he exclaimed at St. Helena, "my life has been!" This romance, made poignant by his stay on that tiny island, was to grow into what came to be known as the Napoleonic Legend, not properly a part of the revolutionary period but destined some day to be a powerful force in the history of nineteenth-century France.

CONCLUSION

Both the Revolution itself and the Napoleonic reforms, especially those of the Consular period, profoundly affected all subsequent aspects of French life. In spite of every storm and stress France still remains a constitutionally ordered republic; the tricolor is its flag; the fourteenth of July (Bastille Day) is its national holiday; the words, "Liberty, Equality, Fraternity," remain its motto; and "the Principles of 1789" are still a rallying cry. Outwardly, it is true, the great monuments of Paris pay greater tribute to Napoleon as the heir of the Revolution than to the earlier leaders, Girondin and Jacobin. Yet, the changes in central and local government, in law, in finances, and in education had their beginning in 1789 and the years immediately following. Napoleon consolidated, enlarged, and disciplined these reforms, thereby providing the essential basis upon which all subsequent structures were to be built.

The dramatic transformation in France had a profound impact abroad. Attitudes began to change, perhaps even more than institutions. The flame of revolutionary nationalism, carried by the republican armies of France, helped to kindle the fires of nationalism in other lands—sometimes in sympathy with the French and sometimes, it is true, in bitter opposition. The effects were to be felt ultimately in Belgium, the Rhineland, Switzerland, Spain, Italy, Prussia, Austria, Russia, and the Balkans. The revolutionary influence reached as far afield as the Spanish colonies in South America where leaders such as Bolivar, Miranda, and San Martin had absorbed the ideas of the French philosophes. San Martin had fought in the French revolutionary armies and had held a general's rank under Napoleon. The law codes of the South American republics were stamped with the ideas of the Napoleonic codes, as were those in many parts of western Europe. New concepts emerged of men as free individuals, new aspirations to win representative institutions, new challenges to ecclesiastical authority, and new attacks upon survivals of feudal privilege. Throughout the nineteenth century Paris stood as the great haven of revolutionary exiles who sought to establish liberal regimes in their homelands.

One further consideration is important. The Bourbon Restoration in France which followed Napoleon's downfall lasted until 1830, when a Paris revolution brought it down. Its uneasy successor, the July Monarchy of the Orléanist Louis Philippe, lasted for eighteen years. Under neither regime was France truly satisfied, and in the turbulent year of 1848 the historic monarchy of France came to its little lamented end. Louis Napoleon, nephew of Napoleon I, was elected president of the Second Republic by an enormous majority. Even the Second Empire which he soon established and then maintained for two decades owed more to the Revolutionary and Napoleonic traditions than it did to the great legacy of France's kings. Moreover, France had to wait until the middle of the nineteenth century to experience the full impact of the Industrial Revolution.

It can well be argued that in the truest sense the phenomenon of revolution persisted for more than a century. While the present volume does not make possible such a lengthy survey, the importance of the larger view should be kept in mind. Not until the Second Empire collapsed in 1870 could the Third Republic begin its troubled history, and not until 1958 was General de Gaulle, in many ways a Napoleonic figure, able to launch still another republic—the Fifth—upon its contemporary course.

BIBLIOGRAPHY

In addition to the general bibliographical works cited in the author's *France—An Interpretive History* (1971) see also P. Caron, *Manuel pratique pour l'étude de la Révolution française* (rev. ed., 1947)."

Abbreviations
AHR: *The American Historical Review*
FHS: *French Historical Studies*
JMH: *The Journal of Modern History*

When more than one date is given, the last is that of the paperback edition, also indicated by an asterisk.

CHAPTER 1: *THE EMERGING CRISIS, 1750–1774*

Some General Works

Friguglietti, J., and Kennedy, E. (eds.), *The Shaping of Modern France: Writings on French History Since 1715* (1969). A selection.
*Gershoy, Leo, *From Despotism to Revolution, 1763–1789* (1944, 1963). In the Langer series.
Gooch, G. P., *Louis XV: The Monarchy in Decline* (1956).
Green, F. C., *Eighteenth Century France* (1964).
Kunstler, C., *La Vie quotidienne sous Louis XV* (1953).
Lough, John (ed.), *An Introduction to Eighteenth Century France* (1960).
*Mitford, Nancy, *Madame de Pompadour* (1968).
Sée, Henri, *Economic and Social Conditions in France During the Eighteenth Century* (Engl. trans., 1931, reissued, 1968).

*Becker, C., *The Heavenly City of the Eighteenth-Century Philosophers* (1932, 1963). A celebrated and provocative essay, evaluated in R. O. Rockwood (ed.), *Carl Becker's Heavenly City Revisited* (1958).

Bien, D., *The Calas Affair* (1960).

*Cassirer, E., *The Philosophy of the Enlightenment* (1932, Engl. trans., 1955). A basic German work.

Cobban, A., *In Search of Humanity. The Role of the Enlightenment in Modern History* (1960).

Crocker, L. B., *Man and the World in Eighteenth Century French Thought* (1959).

Frankel, C., *The Faith of Reason. The Idea of Progress in the French Enlightenment* (1948, reissued, 1969).

*Gay, Peter, *The Enlightenment, an Interpretation,* vol. I, *The Rise of Modern Paganism* (1966, 1968), vol. II, *The Science of Freedom* (1969). A distinguished work.

——, *The Party of Humanity: Essays in the French Enlightenment* (1954).

Hampson, N., *A Cultural History of the Enlightenment* (1969).

*——, *The Enlightenment* (1970).

Havens, G. R., *The Age of Ideas* (1955). Chapters on all major figures.

Hearnshaw, F. J. C. (ed.), *The Social and Political Ideas of Some Great French Thinkers of the Age of Reason* (1950).

*Manuel, F., *The Eighteenth Century Confronts the Gods* (1959, 1967).

*——, *The Prophets of Paris* (1962, 1965). Chapters on Condorcet and Turgot.

*Martin, Kingsley, *French Liberal Thought in the Eighteenth Century* (rev. ed., 1956, 1963).

McCloy, S. T., *French Inventions in the Eighteenth Century* (1952).

Mornet, D., *French Thought in the Eighteenth Century* (1924, Engl. trans., 1969).

——, *Les Origines intellectuelles de la Révolution française* (1933, rev. ed., 1954).

*Palmer, R. R., *Catholics and Unbelievers in Eighteenth Century France* (1939).

Reau, L., *L'Europe française au siècle des lumières* (1951).

Roustan, M., *Pioneers of the French Revolution* (Engl. trans., 1926, reissued, 1969).

Studies of Individuals

Grimsley, R., *Jean D'Alembert, 1717–1783* (1962).

Hankins, T., *Jean D'Alembert: Science and the Enlightenment* (1970).

Knight, Isabel F., *The Geometric Spirit: The Abbé de Condillac and the French Enlightenment* (1968).

Schapiro, J. S., *Condorcet and the Rise of Liberalism* (1934, reissued, 1963).

Crocker, L. G., *The Embattled Philosopher: A Life of Denis Diderot* (1954).

Gillispie, C. C., *Diderot Pictorial Encyclopedia of Trades and Industry* (2 vols., 1959).

Wilson, A. M., *Diderot: The Testing Years 1713–1759* (1957). The first of two projected volumes.

Smith, D. W., *Helvétius: A Study in Persecution* (1965).

Wickwar, W. H., *Baron D'Holbach: A Prelude to the French Revolution* (1935).

Broome, J. H., *Rousseau: A Study of His Thought* (1963).

Cassirer, E., *The Question of Jean-Jacques Rousseau* (Engl. trans., 1954).

*Cobban, A., *Rousseau and the Modern State* (1934, 1964).

Crocker, L. G., *Jean-Jacques Rousseau*, vol. I, *The Quest* (*1712–1758*) (1968).

Green, F. C., *Jean-Jacques Rousseau: A Study of His Life and Writings* (1955).

Grimsley, R., *Jean-Jacques Rousseau: A Study in Self-Awareness* (1961).

———, *Rousseau and the Religious Quest* (1968).

McDonald, Joan, *Rousseau and the French Revolution 1762–1791* (1965).

Shackleton, R., *Montesquieu, A Critical Biography* (1961). The best study.

Dakin, D., *Turgot and the Ancien Régime in France* (1928, reissued, 1965).

Besterman, T., *Voltaire* (1969).

Brumfitt, J. H., *Voltaire, Historian* (1958).

Gay, Peter, *Voltaire's Politics: The Poet as a Realist* (1959).

*Lanson, G., *Voltaire* (1906, 1966). Still one of the best brief surveys.

Maestro, M., *Voltaire and Beccaria as Reformers of Criminal Law* (1942).

Torrey, N., *The Spirit of Voltaire* (1936). Useful essays.

Wade, Ira O., *The Intellectual Development of Voltaire* (1969). A major work.

Waldinger, R., *Voltaire and Reform in the Light of the French Revolution* (1959).

Translations of Contemporary Writings

*Brinton, C. (ed.), *The Portable Age of Reason Reader* (1966).

*Crocker, L. G. (ed.), *The Age of the Enlightenment* (1969).

*Torrey, N. (ed.), *Les Philosophes: The Philosophers of the Enlightenment* (1960).

D'Alembert, *Preliminary Discourse to the Encyclopedia of Diderot*, trans. R. N. Schwab (1968).

Condorcet, *Sketch for a Historical Picture of the Progress of the Human Spirit* (Engl. trans., 1955).

*Descartes, *Discourse on Method and Other Writings*, trans. Wollaston (1968). Essential for background.

*Diderot, *The Encyclopedia: Selections*, trans. S. Gendzier (1967).

*———, *Rameau's Nephew: D'Alembert's Dream*, trans. L. W. Tancock, (1966).

Montesquieu, *Considerations on the Causes of the Greatness of the Romans and Their Decline*, trans. D. Lowenthal (1965).

*———, *The Persian Letters*, trans. G. R. Healy (1964).

*Rousseau, *The Social Contract*, trans. M. Cranston (1968).

*Voltaire, *The Portable Voltaire*, ed. B. R. Raymond (1949).

*———, *The Age of Louis XIV and Other Selected Writings*, trans. J. H. Brumfitt (1963).

*———, *Candide*, trans. J. Butt (1956).

*———, *Philosophical Letters on the English*, trans. E. Dilworth (1961).

*———, *Philosophical Dictionary*, trans. P. Gay (1962).

CHAPTER 2: *FROM REFORM TO REVOLUTION IN FRANCE 1774–1789*

Some General Works

*Behrens, C. B. A., *The Ancien Régime* (1967). Gives the European setting.

Ducros, L., *French Society in the Eighteenth Century* (Engl. trans., 1929).

Green, F. C., *The Ancien Régime: A Manual of French Institutions and Social Classes* (1958).

*Hampson, Norman, *The First European Revolution, 1776–1815* (1969). European in scope.

*Lefebvre, G., *The Coming of the French Revolution* (Engl. trans., 1947, 1957). Important.

Madelin, L., *Le Crépuscule de la monarchie: Louis XVI et Marie-Antoinette* (1936).

*Palmer, R. R., *The Age of the Democratic Revolution*, vol. I, *The Challenge* (1959).

*Sorel, A., *Europe Under the Old Regime* (Engl. trans., 1947, 1963). The first volume of his great work on Europe and the French Revolution.

Taine, H., *The Ancien Régime* (Engl. trans., 1931). A famous work first published in 1875 and severely critical of the "revolutionary spirit."

*Tocqueville, A. de, *The Old Regime and the French Revolution* (Engl. trans., 1955). First published in 1856, arguing that the Revolution succeeded in strengthening what had become an ineffective central power.

Special Aspects

*Barber, E., *The Bourgeoisie in Eighteenth Century France* (1955, 1967).

Behrens, C. B. A., "Nobles, Privileges, and Taxes in France at the End of the Ancien Régime," *Economic History Review*, XV, no. 3 (1963).

Cobban, A., *The Myth of the French Revolution* (1955).

*Church, W. F., *The Influence of the Enlightenment on the French Revolution* (1964). In the *Problems of European Civilization* series.

Egret, Jean, *La Pré-révolution française, 1787–1788* (1962). An important scholarly work.

Eisenstein, E., "Who Intervened in 1788? A Commentary on the Coming of the French Revolution," *AHR*, LXXI (1965). A critique of Lefebvre.

*Ford, Franklin W., *Robe and Sword. The Regrouping of the French Aristocracy After Louis XIV* (1953, 1965).

*———, *Strasbourg in Transition 1648–1789* (1958, 1966). A case study.

Forster, R., *The Nobility of Toulouse in the Eighteenth Century: A Social and Economic Study* (1960).

———, "The Provincial Noble: A Reappraisal," *AHR*, LXVIII (1963).

Garrett, M. B., *The Estates General of 1789* (1935).

*Greenlaw, R., *The Economic Origins of the French Revolution: Poverty or Prosperity?* (1958). In the *Problems in European Civilization* series.

Gruder, V. R., *The Royal Provincial Intendants: A Governing Elite in Eighteenth Century France* (1968).

*Herr, R., *Tocqueville and the Old Regime* (1962).

Hyslop, B., *French Nationalism in 1789 According to the General Cahiers* (1934, reissued, 1968).

*Idzerda, S., *The Background of the French Revolution* (1959). A useful pamphlet.
Kunstler, C., *La Vie quotidienne sous Louis XVI* (1950).
Labrousse, C. E., *La Crise de l'économie française à la fin de l'ancien régime et au début de la Révolution* (1943). A fundamental work.
Matthews, G. T., *The Royal General Farms in Eighteenth Century France* (1958). A study of the indirect taxes.
McCloy, S. T., *Government Assistance in Eighteenth Century France* (1946).
————, *The Humanitarian Movement in Eighteenth Century France* (1957).
*Rothney, J. (ed.), *The Brittany Affair and the Crisis of the Ancien Régime* (1969). In *Problems in European-History* series.
Rudé, G., "The Outbreak of the French Revolution," *Past and Present*, no. 8 (1955).
Shennan, J. H., *The Parlement of Paris* (1968). An important work covering its entire history.
*Young, Arthur, *Travels in France During the Years 1787, 1788, and 1789*, ed. J. Kaplow (1969).

CHAPTER 3: *REFORM AND REVOLUTION 1789-1792*
CHAPTER 4: *THE FIRST FRENCH REPUBLIC 1792-1795*
CHAPTER 5: *THE DIRECTORY AND THE TRIUMPH OF BONAPARTE 1795-1799*

General Histories

*Beik, Paul, *The French Revolution* (1970).
*Brinton, C., *A Decade of Revolution, 1789-1799* (1934, 1963). In the Langer series.
Furet, F., and Richet, D., *La Révolution* (2 vols., 1966, Engl. trans., 1 vol., 1970). Sumptuously illustrated, with a valuable text.
Gershoy, L., *The French Revolution and Napoleon* (1933, new rev. ed., 1964). The best general work in English.
*————, *The Era of the French Revolution, 1789-1799* (1957). A brief outline.
Godechot, J., *France and the Atlantic Revolution of the Eighteenth Century, 1770-1799* (Engl. trans., 1965).
*Goodwin, A., *The French Revolution* (1953, 1960). Goes to 1794.
Hampson, N., *A Social History of the French Revolution* (1963). Useful.
*Hobsbawm, E. J., *The Age of Revolution, 1789-1848* (1962, 1964). A new interpretation.
Kropotkin, P., *The Great French Revolution, 1789-1793* (2 vols., 1909, reissued, 1929). Stresses the class struggle.
Lefebvre, G., *The French Revolution from Its Origins to 1793* (Engl. trans., 1962). This and the following are from the *Peuples et Civilisations* series.
————, *The French Revolution from 1793 to 1799* (Engl. trans., 1964).
*Mathiez, A., *The French Revolution* (Engl. trans., 1928, 1964). Goes to 1794. Strongly Robespierrist.

Pariset, G., *La Révolution, 1792–1799* (1921). In the Lavisse series.
*Rudé, G., *Revolutionary Europe, 1783–1815* (1964, 1965).
Sagnac, P., *La Révolution, 1789–1792* (1920). In the Lavisse series.
Sydenham, M. J., *The French Revolution* (1963).
Thompson, J. M., *The French Revolution* (5th ed., 1955).
Villat, R., *La Révolution et l'Empire, 1789–1815* (2 vols., new ed., 1940–42).

Documents

Anderson, Frank M. (ed.), *Constitutions and Other Select Documents Illustrative of the History of France, 1789–1901* (1904, reissued, 1967).
*Dawson, Philip (ed.), *The French Revolution: Sources* (1967).
Higgins, E. L. (ed.), *The French Revolution as Told by Contemporaries* (1938).
Roberts, J. M. (ed.), *French Revolution Documents*, vol. I (1966).
Stewart, John Hall (ed.), *A Documentary Survey of the French Revolution* (1951, reissued, 1965). Valuable.

Political Aspects

Bienvenu, Richard (ed.), *The Ninth of Thermidor: The Fall of Robespierre* (1968). In the *Problems in European History* series.
Brace, Richard M., *Bordeaux and the Gironde* (1947).
Godfrey, J. R., *Revolutionary Justice: A Study of the Organization, Personnel, and Procedure of the Paris Tribunal, 1793–1795* (1951).
Gooch, R. K., *Parliamentary Government in France: Revolutionary Origins, 1789–1791* (1960).
Goodwin, A., "The French Executive Directory — A Revaluation," *History*, XXII, no. 87 (1937). Emphasizes the constructive aspects.
Kerr, W. B., *The Reign of Terror 1793–1794* (1927).
Lefebvre, G., *The Thermidoreans and the Directory: Two Phases of the French Revolution* (Engl. trans., 1964).
Lokke, C. L., *France and the Colonial Question 1763–1801* (1932).
*Mathiez, A., *After Robespierre: The Thermidorean Reaction* (Engl. trans., 1931, 1965).
———, *The Fall of Robespierre and Other Essays* (Engl. trans., 1927, reissued, 1970).
Moore, James M., *The Roots of French Republicanism: The Evolution of the Republican Ideal and Its Culmination in the Constitution of 1793* (1962). A substantial work.
*Palmer, R. R., *Twelve Who Ruled: The Committee of Public Safety During the Terror* (1941, 1970).
Paret, P., *Internal War and Pacification: The Vendée, 1789–1796* (1961).
Sirich, J. B., *The Revolutionary Committees in the Departments of France, 1793–1794* (1943).
Sydenham, M. J., *The Girondins* (1961). Challenges the romantic view of this group.
Thompson, E., *Popular Sovereignty and the French Constituent Assembly, 1789–1791* (1952).
Tilly, C., *The Vendée* (1964).

Social and Economic Aspects

Brinton, C., *The Jacobins, an Essay in the New History* (1930, reissued, 1961). Still the most useful study.

Clough, S. B., *France, A History of National Economics, 1789–1939* (1939, reissued, 1964).

Davies, A., "The Origins of the Peasant Revolution of 1789," *History*, XLIX (1964).

Elliott, Sir John, *The Way of the Tumbrils* (1958).

Godechot, J., *The Taking of the Bastille* (Engl. trans., 1970). A definitive study with important background.

Greer, Donald, *The Incidence of the Terror During the French Revolution* (1935). Greer's statistical methods are criticized by R. Louie, "The Incidence of the Terror: A Critique of Statistical Interpretation," *FHS*, III (1964).

———, *The Incidence of the Emigration During the French Revolution* (1951).

Harris, Seymour E., *The Assignats* (1930, reissued, 1969).

Hearnshaw, F. J. C. (ed.), *The Social and Political Ideas of Some Representative Thinkers of the Revolutionary Era* (1931).

Loomis, S., *Paris in the Terror: June 1793–July 1794* (1964). Popular.

Palmer, R. R., "Popular Democracy in the French Revolution," *FHS*, I (1960).

———, "George Lefebvre: The Peasants and the French Revolution," *JMH*, XXI (1959).

Robiquet, J., *Daily Life in the French Revolution* (Engl. trans., 1965).

Rose, R. B., *The Enragés: Socialists of the French Revolution?* (Melbourne, 1965).

*Rudé, G., *The Crowd in the French Revolution* (1967). An outstanding example of the new statistical approach.

———, "Prices, Wages and Popular Movements During the French Revolution," *Economic History Review*, VI (1954).

Shepard, W. F., *Price Control and the Reign of Terror: France, 1793–1795* (1953).

*Soboul, A., *The Parisian Sans-Culottes and the French Revolution, 1793–1794* (Engl. trans., abridged, 1964).

Thomson, David, *The Babeuf Plot: The Making of a Republican Legend* (1947).

*Williams, Gwyn A., *Artisans and Sans-Culottes: Popular Movements in France and Britain During the French Revolution* (1961).

Diplomatic and Military

Biro, S., *The German Policy of Revolutionary France* (2 vols., 1957).

Godechot, J., *La Grande Nation: l'expansion révolutionnaire de la France dans le monde de 1789 à 1799* (2 vols., 1956). Treats the Revolution as part of a much wider popular unrest.

Gooch, G. P., *Germany and the French Revolution* (1920, reissued, 1966).

Heriot, A., *The French in Italy, 1796–1799* (1957).

Laprade, W. T., *England and the French Revolution, 1789–1797* (1909, re-issued, 1970).

Mahan, A. T., *The Influence of Sea Power upon the French Revolution and the Empire 1793–1812* (2 vols., 1893, and many later editions).

McClellan, G. B., *Venice and Bonaparte* (1931).

*Palmer, R. R., *The Age of the Democratic Revolution*, vol. II, *The Struggle* (1964). Fundamental for the "sister republics."

Wilkinson, S., *The French Army Before Napoleon* (1915).

Cultural Aspects

Barnard, H. C., *Education and the French Revolution* (1969).

Carlson, M., *The Theater of the French Revolution* (1966).

Dowd, D., *Pageant-Master of the Republic: Jacques-Louis David and the French Revolution* (1948).

——, "The French Revolution and the Painters," *FHS*, I (1959).

Guerlac, H., "Some Aspects of Science During the French Revolution," *The Scientific Monthly*, 80 (1955).

Helmreich, Jonathan, "The Establishment of Primary Schools in France Under the Directory," *FHS*, II (1961).

Hyslop, Beatrice F., "The Theater During a Crisis: The Paris Theater During the Reign of Terror," *JMH*, XVII (1945).

Idzerda, S. J., "Iconoclasm During the French Revolution," *AHR*, LIX (1954).

Leith, James A., *The Idea of Art as Propaganda in France, 1750–1799: A Study in the History of Ideas* (1965).

Parker, H. T., *The Cult of Antiquity and the French Revolutionaries* (1937, reissued, 1965).

Rogers, Cornwell B., *The Spirit of Revolution in 1789: A Study of Public Opinion as Revealed in Political Songs and Other Popular Literature* (1949).

Vignery, J. R., *The French Revolution and the Schools: Educational Policies of the Mountain, 1792–1794* (1965).

Williams, L. P., "Science, Education and the French Revolution," *Isis*, XLIV (1953).

Religion

Andrews, G. G., "Making the Revolutionary Calendar," *AHR*, XXVI (1932).

Aulard, A., *Christianity and the French Revolution* (Engl. trans., 1927). Highly critical of the Church.

Dansette, A., *A Religious History of Modern France* (Engl. trans., 1961).

McManners, J., *The French Revolution and the Church* (1970).

Poland, B. C., *French Protestantism and the French Revolution: A Study in Church and State, Thought and Religion, 1685–1815* (1957).

Interpretative

*Amann, P., *The Eighteenth Century Revolution, French or Western?* (1963).
In the *Problems in European Civilization* series.
Beik, P., *The French Revolution as Seen From the Right* (1956).
*Brinton, C., *The Anatomy of Revolution* (1938, 1957). A comparative study
of four revolutions.
Cobb, R., *The French Revolution in Historical Thought* (1967).
Cobban, A., *The Debate on the French Revolution* (2nd ed., 1960).
*————, *The Social Interpretation of the French Revolution* (1964, 1968).
Ford, Franklin D., "The Revolutionary-Napoleonic Era: How Much of a
Watershed?" *AHR*, LXIX (1963).
*Kafker, F. A., and Laux, J. M. (eds.), *The French Revolution, Conflicting
Interpretations* (1968).
*Kaplow, J. (ed.), *New Perspectives on the French Revolution: Readings in
Historical Sociology* (1965).
Palmer, R. R., "Reflections on the French Revolution," *Political Science
Quarterly*, LXVII (1952).
Rudé, G., *Interpretations of the French Revolution* (1961).

Biographies

Madelin, L., *Figures of the Revolution* (Engl. trans., 1968).
*Thompson, J. M., *Leaders of the French Revolution* (1929, 1962).
Whitham, J. M., *A Biographical History of the French Revolution* (1931).

Brucker, G. A., *Jean-Sylvain Bailly, Revolutionary Mayor of Paris* (1950).
Gershoy, L., *Bertrand Barère, A Reluctant Terrorist* (1962).
Bradley, E. D., *Life of Barnave* (2 vols., 1915).
Ellery, E., *Brissot de Warville* (1915).
Dupré, H., *Lazare Carnot, Republican Patriot* (1940).
Watson, S. J., *Carnot, 1753–1823* (1954).
Schapiro, J. S., *Condorcet and the Rise of Liberalism* (1934).
Madelin, L., *Danton* (Engl. trans., 1923).
Morton, J. B., *Camille Desmoulins* (1951).
Zweig, S., *Joseph Fouché* (Engl. trans., 1930).
Gottschalk, Louis, The fifth volume of his monumental *Lafayette* (1969)
brings the story to October 1789.
————, *Jean Paul Marat, a Study in Radicalism* (1927, new ed., 1967).
Castelot, A., *Queen of France* [Marie Antoinette] (Engl. trans., 1957).
Welch, O. J. G., *Mirabeau: A Study of a Democratic Monarchist* (1951,
new ed., 1968).
Robison, G., *Revellière-Lepeaux, Citizen Director* (1938).
Thompson, J. M., *Robespierre* (2 vols., 1936, reissued, 1968).
*————, *Robespierre and the French Revolution* (1953). A sketch.
May, Gita, *Madame Roland and the Age of Revolution* (1970).
Bruun, G., *Saint-Just, Apostle of the Terror* (1932, reissued, 1966).
Curtis, E. N., *Saint-Just, Colleague of Robespierre* (1935).
Van Deusen, G. G., *Sieyès: His Life and His Nationalism* (1932).

Herold, J. C., *Mistress to an Age: A Life of Madame de Staël* (1958).
*Brinton, C., *The Lives of Talleyrand* (1936, 1963).
*Duff-Cooper, A., *Talleyrand* (1932, 1967).
Bowers, C. G., *Pierre Vergniaud* (1951).

CHAPTER 6: *NAPOLEONIC FRANCE*
CHAPTER 7: *NAPOLEONIC EUROPE*

General Histories and Sources

*Bruun, G., *Europe and the French Imperium* (rev. ed., 1957, 1963). In the Langer series. Valuable for its broad interpretations.
Crawley, C. W. (ed.), *War and Peace in an Age of Upheaval, 1789–1830*, vol. IX, *The New Cambridge Modern History* (1965).
*Godechot, J., Hyslop, B. F., and Dowd, D. L., *The Napoleonic Era in Europe* (1970).
Herold, J. C., *The Horizon Book of the Age of Napoleon* (1963). Lavishly illustrated.
"La France à l'époque Napoléonienne," *Revue d'histoire moderne et contemporaine*, XVII (July–September, 1970). Devoted to substantial articles on the Napoleonic period.
Lefebvre, G., *Napoléon* (5th rev. ed., 1965, Engl. trans., 2 vols., 1969). The most complete treatment of the period, in the *Peuples et Civilisations* series.
Madelin, L., *The Consulate and the Empire* (2 vols., Engl. trans., 1921). Strongly Bonapartist.
Mistler, J. (ed.), *Napoléon et l'Empire* (2 vols., 1969). Sumptuously illustrated, with authoritative articles.
Pariset, G., *Le Consulat et l'Empire* (1921). In the Lavisse series.
De Chair, S. (ed.), *Napoleon's Memoirs* (1950).
Howard, J. E. (trans.), *Letters and Documents of Napoleon Bonaparte*, vol. I, *The Rise to Power* (1961). The first of three projected volumes.

Biographies of Napoleon

Bainville, J., *Napoleon* (Engl. trans., 1931, new illustr. ed., 1970). Popular and sound.
*Butterfield, *Napoleon* (1939, 1966). Brief.
*Fisher, H. A. L., *Napoleon* (1912, 1967).
Fournier, A., *Napoleon* (Engl. trans., 1925).
Kircheisen, F. M., *Napoleon* (Engl. trans., 1932). An abridgment of the nine German volumes, 1911–34).
*Markham, F., *Napoleon* (1963, 1966). The best work in English.
*———, *Napoleon and the Awakening of Europe* (1965). A shorter version.
Rose, J. H., *Life of Napoleon the First* (1901). Long the standard English life and still useful.
Thompson, J. M., *Napoleon Bonaparte: His Rise and Fall* (1952).

Administrative Reforms

Artz, F. B., *The Development of Technical Education in France, 1500–1815* (1967).
Biver, Countess M. L., *Le Paris de Napoléon* (1963). Documented and substantial.
Higby, C. P., and Willis, C. B., "Industry and Labor Under Napoleon," *AHR*, LIII (1948).
*Holtman, R. B., *The Napoleonic Revolution* (1967). Very useful series of essays.
———, *Napoleonic Propaganda* (1950).
Fisher, H. A. L., *Bonapartism* (1914, reissued, 1957).
Melvin, Frank E., *Napoleon's Navigation System* (1919).
Ponteil, F., *Napoléon I et l'organisation autoritaire de la France* (1956). Indispensable.
Williams, L. P., "Science and Napoleon," *Isis*, XLVII (1956).

Military

Adlow, E., *Napoleon in Italy 1796–1797* (1931).
Chandler, David G., *The Campaigns of Napoleon* (1966).
Earle, E. M. (ed.), *Makers of Modern Strategy* (1943).
Esposito, V. J. and Elting, J. C., *A Military History and Atlas of the Napoleonic Wars* (1964).
Herold, J. C., *Napoleon in Egypt* (1962).
MacDonnell, A. G., *Napoleon and His Marshals* (1934).
Naylor, J., *Waterloo* (1960).
Ross, S. T., "The Military Strategy of the Directory: The Campaigns of 1798," *FHS*, V (1967).
Quimby, R. S., *The Background of Napoleonic Warfare* (1957).
Tarle, E. V., *Napoleon's Invasion of Russia* (Engl. trans., 1942). By a Soviet historian.

Foreign Affairs

Butterfield, H., *The Peace Tactics of Napoleon 1806–1808* (1929).
Connelly, O. S., *The Gentle Bonaparte* [Joseph] (1968).
———, *Napoleon's Satellite Kingdoms* (1965).
Dard, E., *Napoleon and Talleyrand* (Engl. trans., 1937).
Deutsch, H., *The Genesis of Napoleonic Imperialism* (1938).
Kissinger, Henry, *A World Restored* (1957). The 1815 settlement.
Lovett, G. H., *Napoleon and the Birth of Modern Spain* (2 vols., 1965).
Lyon, E. W., *Louisiana in French Diplomacy 1759–1804* (1934).
Mowat, R. B., *The Diplomacy of Napoleon* (1924). Based on Sorel's great work.
Puryear, V. J., *Napoleon and the Dardanelles* (1951).
Rath, R. J., *The Fall of the Napoleonic Kingdom of Italy* (1941).
Schmitt, H. A., "Stein, Alexander, and the Crusade Against Napoleon," *JMH*, XXI (1959).
Scott, F. D., *Bernadotte and the Fall of Napoleon* (1935).

Shupp, Paul F., *The European Powers and the Near Eastern Question, 1806–1807* (1929).
Sorel, A., *Napoleon and the French Revolution, 1799–1814* (Engl. trans., 1928). Excerpts from his eight-volume work.

Religion

Dansette, cited in ch. XVI.
Hales, E. E. Y., *Napoleon and the Pope: The Story of Napoleon and Pius VII* (1961).
Walsh, H. H., *The Concordat of 1801* (1933).

St. Helena

Aubry, O., *St Helena* (Engl. trans., 1937).
Bertrand, H. G., *Cahiers de Sainte-Hélène* (3 vols., 1949–59). A mine of information.
Guérard, A., *Reflections on the Napoleonic Legend* (1924).
Korngold, R., *The Last Years of Napoleon* (1959).
Martineau, G., *Napoleon's St. Helena* (Engl. trans., 1969).
Rosebery, Lord, *Napoleon: The Last Phase* (1900, and later eds.). A famous work.

Miscellaneous

Andrews, G. G., *Napoleon in Review* (1939).
Aronson, T., *The Golden Bees: The Story of the Bonapartes* (1964).
*Geyl, P., *Napoleon—For and Against* (1949, 1967). An evaluation of the chief Napoleonic historians.
Goodspeed, D. J., *Napoleon's Eighty Days* (1965). The coup of Brumaire.
Healy, F. G., *The Literary Culture of Napoleon* (1959).
*Herold, J. C. (ed.), *The Mind of Napoleon. A Selection of His Written and Spoken Words* (1955, 1961).
Kemble, J., *Napoleon Immortal* (1959). A medical history.
*Knapton, E. J., *Empress Josephine* (1963, 1969).
Lefebvre, G., *Napoleon from 18 Brumaire to Tilsit, 1799–1807* (Engl. trans., 1969).
Kohn, H., "Napoleon and the Age of Nationalism," *JMH*, XXII (1950).
Morton, J. B., *Brumaire: The Rise of Bonaparte* (1944).
*Pinkney, D. H., *Napoleon: Historical Enigma* (1969). In the *Problems in European Civilization* series.
Quynn, D. M., "The Art Confiscations of the Napoleonic Wars," *AHR*, L (1945).
Weiner, Margery, *The Parvenu Princesses: Elisa, Pauline and Caroline Bonaparte* (1964).
Wright, Constance, *Daughter to Napoleon: A Biography of Hortense, Queen of Holland* (1961).

INDEX